50 A$KS

in 50 Weeks

Second Edition

A Guide to Better Fundraising for Your Small Development Shop

Amy Eisenstein, MPA, ACFRE

*Charity*Channel®
P R E S S ™

50 Asks in 50 Weeks: A Guide to Better Fundraising for Your Small Development Shop, Second Edition

One of the **In the Trenches**™ series

Published by

CharityChannel Press, an imprint of CharityChannel LLC

424 Church Street, Suite 2000

Nashville, TN 37219 USA

CharityChannel.com

ISBN Print Book: 978-1-938077-91-3 | ISBN eBook: 978-1-938077-92-0

Library of Congress Control Number: 2016949722

13 12 11 10 9 8 7 6 5 4 3 2 1

Printed in the United States of America

This and most CharityChannel Press books are available at special quantity discounts for bulk purchases for sales promotions, premiums, fundraising, or educational use. For information, contact CharityChannel Press, 424 Church Street, Suite 2000, Nashville, TN 37219 USA. +1 949-589-5938.

Publisher's Acknowledgments

This book was produced by a team dedicated to excellence; please send your feedback to Editors@ CharityChannel.com.

We first wish to acknowledge the tens of thousands of peers who call *CharityChannel.com* their online professional home. Your enthusiastic support for the **In the Trenches**™ series is the wind in our sails.

Members of the team who produced this book include:

Editors

Acquisitions: Stephen C. Nill

Comprehensive Editing: Rebecca St. Andrie

Copy Editing: Stephen C. Nill

Production

Layout: Stephen C. Nill

Design: Deborah Perdue

Administrative

CharityChannel LLC: Stephen Nill, CEO

Marketing and Public Relations: John Millen

About the Author

Amy Eisenstein, MPA, ACFRE is an author, speaker, trainer, and consultant. Her published books include *Major Gift Fundraising for Small Shops, Raising More with Less,* and *50 Asks in 50 Weeks.*

She is a frequent speaker at national and local conferences as well as at staff and board retreats on a variety of topics. She became an Association of Fundraising Professionals (AFP) certified Master Trainer in 2009.

Amy recently completed her service as the president of the board of the Association of Fundraising Professionals—New Jersey Chapter.

She became a Certified Fundraising Executive (CFRE) in 2004 and received her advanced certification, ACFRE, in 2013.

Amy regularly blogs and vlogs at amyeisenstein.com.

Dedication

This book is dedicated to all the hardworking nonprofit staff and board members who are committed to making the world a better place. Best wishes for your fundraising success!

Author's Acknowledgments

Many thanks to my friends and colleagues who are in the fundraising trenches, especially those who have been using *50 Asks in 50 Weeks* since the first edition in 2010. I appreciate your support, encouragement, and enthusiasm along the way.

A special thank you to Dawn Wolfe, who helped to significantly improve and enrich this work. It is a much better book thanks to your hard work and encouragement.

Thank you to Stephen Nill, Founder and CEO of CharityChannel, for encouraging me to write a second edition of *50 Asks in 50 Weeks*.

AFP has provided me with quality, ongoing fundraising education over the last two decades and is where I learned the basics at the beginning of my fundraising career. Thanks, also, to all of my friends and colleagues at the New Jersey chapter of AFP.

And most importantly, I would like to express my heartfelt gratitude to my family and friends who have supported me and my career over the years, especially my husband Alan and our children Ethan and Zoe. Finally, thanks to Goldie the Goldendoodle, who has brought countless hours of joy to our lives.

Contents

Summary of Chapters

Grant Research, Writing, and Relationships. Though popular with small nonprofits, the truth is only a small percentage of philanthropic dollars available come from grants. Yet, grant seeking can be helpful, as long as your organization is not relying too heavily on it. I cover the basics.

Events Aren't About Ticket Sales, They're About Sponsorship. I'm convinced that all nonprofits should have at least one fundraising event every year. Even so, there are significant drawbacks that we'll cover.

For Executive Directors Only. Are you an executive director? If you've read this workbook chapter by chapter, you already know that you're critical to your organization's fundraising success. If you're starting with this chapter, know this: fundraising should take half your time. Really.

Putting it All Together: Keys to Success. We discuss how to stay on track, follow your plan, and count and measure your success. Yes, *your success!*

Foreword

This may have been the easiest "yes" in my life.

Besides the fact that it was a huge honor to be asked to write the Foreword to the Second Edition of *50 Asks in 50 Weeks*, the request involved the intersection of three loves for me.

◆ I love fundraising.

◆ I love *50 Asks*.

◆ I love Amy.

First, there's the love of fundraising. Like Amy, I never imagined I'd have a career in fundraising. But once I got a taste of it, I couldn't stop. *50 Asks* will infect you with that same passion. And equip you to succeed.

Next, I love the book. From the time I read the first edition, I have been filled with admiration for the practical, useful, achievable steps Amy offers her readers. This second edition builds on the same actionable approach and adds even more in the areas of time management, donor stewardship, online giving, and major gifts. Somehow Amy has taken a great book and made it better!

Third, you can't know Amy Eisenstein and not love her. From the time we first met (she doesn't remember, and I can't forget!) I knew Amy was a winner and would become a leader in our profession. I couldn't have guessed how rapidly it would happen. As you read the pages that follow, you'll understand why fundraisers from around the globe lean to the front edge of their chair whenever she speaks. Amy brings a refreshing clarity to the complexity of fundraising excellence. She makes success attainable for new and experienced fundraisers alike.

Because of her robust experience with charities of all stripes, Amy is uniquely positioned to equip others to move from maintenance mode to high impact. She jumps right in and clarifies exactly what is meant by the term, "Ask." Rather than water it down to a level that would strip the word of significance, Amy defines "the Ask" for exactly what it is. With this definition in hand, she makes everything else in the book relevant.

Amy baits the audience to read and apply her concepts by offering a bold promise. She claims *50 Asks* will prepare fundraisers to become "more confident and comfortable asking others" for money. I have only two words in response to this offer. *Promise delivered!*

Perhaps Amy's most salient advice in *50 Asks* is her gentle but firm nudge that will free the flow of funds into your organization. "Successful fundraising," she says, "requires you to take action, including getting out of your chair, picking up your phone, and meeting with donors." I heartily agree.

I have only two complaints with *50 Asks in 50 Weeks*:

1. I wish Amy had written the book thirty years earlier. Why? The explanation is really quite simple. Even after decades of successful fundraising experience, the nuggets of truth I discovered in *50 Asks* would most certainly have catapulted my career forward beyond what all the other resources have.

2. One particular example comes to mind. Amy unfolds the secrets of delegation and reveals how fundraisers benefit everyone when they artfully employ this practice. This one tip is easily worth a thousand times the cost of the book!

The words "For The Small Shop" should be removed from the cover. Yes, *50 Asks* is spot-on for all who are involved in fundraising at smaller organizations. But I've read the book. And I've worked with organizations that are larger and more sophisticated. So here's what I want to say about that: Every principle Amy presents is equally applicable to these other charities. And many fundraisers operating in such environments would benefit greatly from Amy's wise counsel.

As you can see, my "complaints" are offered tongue in cheek, and I heartily commend this new edition to you and your colleagues, whether paid professionals or volunteers. My sincere hope is that *50 Asks in 50 Weeks* will be as beneficial to you and those you serve as it has been for me.

M. Kent Stroman, CFRE

Author, *Asking About Asking* and *The Intentional Board*
Keynote speaker on philanthropy and governance
Founder, The Institute for Conversational Fundraising

Introduction

For almost twenty years I have helped nonprofit organizations raise millions of dollars to change and save lives.

But believe it or not, I started out hating even the *idea* of asking for money! While I was in graduate school, thinking of fundraising evoked visions of cold calls, clammy hands, and begging.

I was studying public administration and nonprofit management in graduate school, and I thought that my eventual goal was to be the executive director of a nonprofit. I knew that to get there, I would need to either raise money myself or supervise other fundraisers. (What I didn't quite understand then is that fundraising is *also* an integral part of being an executive director!)

To get my much-dreaded fundraising experience out of the way, I applied for my first fundraising job—thinking of it as a necessary evil on the way to nonprofit leadership.

Imagine my surprise when I fell in love with fundraising!

Today, I'm grateful for a career of almost twenty years of direct fundraising experience (no clammy hands or "begging" involved) as a director of development, and then as a consultant, to many important nonprofit organizations.

I'm also thrilled to have the opportunity to share what my clients and I have learned together through my blog and in books like the one you hold in your hands.

Why does raising money mean so much to me? Because fundraising isn't about the money! Nonprofits live, die, or muddle along depending on their fundraising abilities (or lack thereof), which means that fundraising success determines just how effective they will be in serving their mission.

In other words, fundraising *is* necessary—but it's far from evil!

In fact, I can't imagine a bigger thrill than successfully closing a gift and knowing that I have just been part of continuing, or even expanding, an organization's ability to change lives and save lives.

By the end of this book I hope you love raising money as much as I do; at the very least, I believe that you'll come away feeling more confident and comfortable asking others for the funds your organization needs.

The first step toward developing a love of (or at least comfort with) fundraising is to realize just what professional fundraising is and what it is not.

When you ask another person for a donation, you're *not* "begging" for money. Instead, you're providing them with the opportunity to invest in a cause that they care about and to do something positive for the wider community.

It doesn't matter whether the issue is education, homelessness, the environment, healthcare, seniors, children, people with disabilities, or a host of other worthy, important causes. As a fundraising professional, executive director, or board member, *you're part of the solution* when you ask others to give.

So let's get started, shall we?

Why Aren't You Raising the Money Your Cause Deserves?

There are many reasons why nonprofit professionals and volunteers don't raise as much money as they could (or should). For one, many fundraisers and executive directors are overworked, leaving them limited time and resources (not to mention energy) to devote to raising money.

Another reason is that most people working in fundraising don't have any formal training, and therefore don't have the necessary skills or expertise to raise funds effectively and efficiently.

Fundraising is a lot of work, and it takes a team of people working together to get the job done. If your organization expects the development or executive director alone to be responsible for your bottom line, you're not being nearly as effective as you can (and should) be!

Changing Times Call for a Change in Strategy

When I started out in this business fundraising was relatively easy. Throughout the 1990s and even the beginning in the 2000s, in fact, the money was flowing.

Of course, today that's no longer the case—and it hasn't been for many years now. Successful fundraising requires you to take action, including getting out of your chair, picking up your phone, and meeting with donors.

That said, there *is* good news—according to Giving USA's *Annual Report on Philanthropy* for 2015, nonprofit giving overall increased by 4.1 percent. If that doesn't sound like much, think of it this way— 2015's total nonprofit giving added up to $373 *billion*.

However, it's still necessary to get out there and take positive action to increase your organization's bottom line. Taking action to raise money, and doing it efficiently and effectively, is what this second edition of *50 Asks in 50 Weeks* is all about.

Another reason you may not be raising the kind of money you could involves the ways you *are* spending your time. This isn't just about being overworked (though that's part of it). Frequently, "asking for gifts" falls to the bottom of a long list of urgent, but ultimately less important, work.

Even experienced fundraisers can get sidetracked with tasks ranging from event planning to managing the database or writing thank-you letters. While extremely important, these tasks (among many others) don't lead *directly* to any additional income for the organization.

To raise more money, you must move asking back to the top of your priority list.

Simple Changes Bring Big Results

My first experience asking for money happened during my very first fundraising job at a battered women's shelter. (This was the job that would supposedly get fundraising "out of the way" so I could get on with my "real" career as an executive director.)

I was still in graduate school at the time and learning about fundraising theory—now I was going to put my knowledge into practice.

When I arrived, the shelter was doing what I call "bake sale" and "car wash" fundraising: their efforts relied on several labor-intensive projects that didn't make much money.

In addition to their "bake sale" efforts the shelter received a few private grants, but the majority of its funding came from government sources. With a few simple, but important changes, we were able to develop a small individual giving program, sponsorship opportunities, and a direct mail program—all of which made a significant impact on our bottom line.

stories from the real world

If the story of my first fundraising job in the sidebar above sounds familiar, don't worry! That means that yours is one of many nonprofits that are operating the same way.

With the help of this book, you can and will take your organization to the next level.

The second edition of *50 Asks in 50 Weeks* is a development planning workbook. By the time you've finished it you will have created a basic annual development plan by focusing on three important subjects:

◆ The significance of asking for gifts frequently

◆ The importance of having a diverse funding base

◆ The impact of asking in the smartest possible way

I've chosen these three subjects (instead of just the first) because, although the focus of the concept of *50 Asks in 50 Weeks* is on asking more frequently, I certainly recognize the risk of not having a diversified donor base. There's also danger in focusing too much on frequency—doing so leads to making the kinds of mistakes that actually result in a *decrease* in gifts.

After all, the ultimate goal is to raise more money and create a more stable donor base, not just to ask more frequently.

Why Fifty Asks?

In my experience, the staff members in average, small development offices make far fewer than fifty asks per year—and receive far fewer gifts.

The Ask

An *ask* is the actual solicitation in the fundraising process. I use the term to refer to any request for money including a grant application, event invitation, appeal letter, and sponsorship request, as well as an individual, face-to-face solicitation.

definition

(My definition of a small development shop is an organization with a budget of under $3 million, and/or less than three paid development staff members. This includes a "zero" development staff shop, which is an organization with no paid development staff member and where the executive director, program staff, and/or volunteers are responsible for all the fundraising.)

While fifty is a somewhat arbitrary number, then, it still represents a marked increase over what most small-development-staff shops are doing now. Most importantly, it's an *achievable* number.

50 Asks in 50 Weeks is uniquely aimed to help your small development office raise significantly more fundraising revenue while building skills as a generalist in our field.

I've designed this workbook specifically to help you make a huge leap in your fundraising income—something that shouldn't be difficult once you realize that you're not asking for gifts nearly as often as you could.

Once you've put your plan into action, I urge you to contact me with the results: both successes and setbacks. Let me know what has worked well for you and what hasn't worked as well as you'd like. Your experiences may well make it into the next edition!

Best wishes for your fundraising success!

Thank you,

Amy Eisenstein, MPA, ACFRE

Chapter One

Getting Started: What You Need to Know to Get to Fifty Asks

IN THIS CHAPTER

- ┅► How to define and count your asks

- ┅► The keys to success: frequency, diversity, and efficiency

- ┅► The case for support and how to create a strong one

- ┅► The fundraising cycle

N o doubt about it. Making more frequent asks will increase your nonprofit's bottom line. But there are a number of things you need to know first. This chapter is about those concepts. Whether you're using *50 Asks in 50 Weeks* to create your first fundraising plan or simply to refresh yourself on the principles, start here.

Paying more attention to how frequently you're asking is vital. Why? Because most small organizations aren't making as many asks as they can—and wondering why they're not raising enough money! Focusing on the number of asks you're making will give you an easy benchmark to see if your fundraising efforts are growing each year.

In my experience, most nonprofits with small development shops (three or fewer paid fundraising staff members) are asking at most twenty to thirty times per year using the counting method I've outlined below. Also, I assume that you're not receiving all the gifts you *do* ask for. If on the other hand, you *are* receiving every gift you ask for, I can virtually guarantee you're certainly not asking frequently enough—or for enough money!

Regardless of the response rate on your asks, if you're like the majority you almost certainly have the potential to raise significantly more money with the right plan in place.

The first part of the plan includes asking much more often. The second ensures you are asking effectively and efficiently.

Counting Your Asks

Since we are focusing on frequency of asking as a key to successful fundraising, it's important to learn to count the number of asks you make each year.

Why am I including a discussion about how to count your asks? Because whenever I speak at a conference or meeting, I'm always asked whether this, that, or the other thing "counts" as an ask. For example, do you count asking each board member separately, or count them as one because it's a group?

Here's the bottom line: Whether you decide to use my system for counting or your own isn't important. What *is* important is staying consistent in the way you count from year to year.

Throughout this workbook (and online) you'll find worksheets to help you list your asks. The total you come up with will be the benchmark you use to increase your asks this year, next year, and in years to come.

Feel free to skip to the end of the chapter and count your asks now.

The Importance of a Diverse Funding Base

In addition to asking frequently, another key to a successful development program is to ensure you have a *diversified funding base.* This means that you have multiple revenue streams coming from a variety of sources.

Diversified Funding Base

A *diversified funding base* means that you have multiple revenue streams coming from a variety of sources.

A well-balanced portfolio of donors is crucial to the safety and financial security of any nonprofit. Your organization should have a variety of donors of differing size and scope in each of the following areas: foundations, corporations, individuals, and possibly government support at the federal, state, or local level.

It's also important to generate income in a variety of ways. This includes individual solicitations, bulk mail, fundraising events, grant writing, and even earned income. (Earned income, or "social enterprise," is a huge topic that's beyond the scope of this workbook. A very short explanation includes providing goods or services in exchange for a fee, such as a class at a YMCA.)

A diverse funding base is so critically important because organizations that rely on single sources of income put themselves, their programs, and the people or causes they serve in jeopardy as soon as any major funding source is eliminated.

An organization also needs a diverse funding base because most funders don't *want* to be the lone supporter of an entire program or organization. This is true for a variety of reasons, including:

◆ Most funders want to be able to spread their resources around a variety of organizations, not spend all their available philanthropy dollars on one agency.

◆ Most funders don't want a program (or agency) to be completely dependent on their individual gifts because they don't want the burden of feeling completely responsible for its continued existence.

◆ Most funders don't want to take big risks. They feel more comfortable when they join others in supporting a particular program or organization; the more funders there are, the more stable it is. Also, money attracts money. If several organizations are investing in your nonprofit, that level of support is in itself a marketing tool.

◆ Most funders don't want to invest their money in a "sinking ship." It's important to be confident in your organization and not come at funders from a place of desperation. Very, very few people are willing to "save" an organization—and *no one* wants to feel as though they're throwing their money away.

The Danger of Relying on a Single Funder

When I started consulting in 2008, I received many calls from organizations that were heavily reliant on government funding. Often up to 90 percent of their funding was from government sources. They were terrified that if (and when) their funding was cut, their entire organization would be eliminated. How could they possibly make up 90 percent of their funding? It's a scary position to be in, which is why having a diversified funding base is so critical.

stories from the real world

It doesn't matter how dedicated your current funders are. Individuals suffer personal setbacks, foundations change their priorities, and since the "Great Recession" started in 2008, government funding is being cut all the time.

But if you follow the *50 Asks in 50 Weeks* plan, you can help ensure that your organization receives money from a wide variety of sources and will remain stable in the inevitable event that one (or more) of those sources dries up.

Asking Smart

The old saying, "Quality, not quantity," also rings true in fundraising. It's more important to make smart, informed asks than to make a certain number of asks each year. So although increasing your overall number of asks is crucial, more asks alone aren't enough. Prospective donors—whether foundations, corporations, or individuals—must be carefully researched, cultivated, solicited, and stewarded.

If you ask one hundred times a year but don't receive any gifts, frequency becomes irrelevant. It's the number of gifts you *receive*, not the number of gifts you ask for, that truly counts. Unproductive fundraising is a waste of everyone's time.

When Asking Isn't Smart

When I started my job at a battered women's shelter, one of the first projects I was asked to work on was a Valentine's Day card sale. This was the shelter's annual fundraiser and consisted of having board members and other volunteers sell Valentine's Day cards at busy train stations around the area. The shelter only netted a few dollars per box, but staff and volunteers put a tremendous amount of energy into selling each one. Not only that, but we were primarily selling the cards for cash to people who would never be added to our mailing list—and who probably didn't know or care much about the cause. Clearly, the card sale was way too much effort for far too little return. Unfortunately, the board and staff were so reliant on the small infusion of unrestricted cash the sale brought in each winter that they were extremely reluctant to give it up.

stories from the real world

My first employer's Valentine's Day card sale (see the sidebar on the previous page) was a perfect example of unproductive fundraising. In its place, we ended up instituting four new initiatives, each of which raised the profile of the shelter in the community *and* raised many more dollars without too much additional effort.

This is what we did:

◆ We created a newsletter with a business reply envelope. Until this newsletter, donors only heard from the shelter in the form of an annual appeal letter, once a year. Although the first newsletter only resulted in about ten responses, each of those envelopes had an average of $50—which meant we raised $500 while at the same time raising awareness about our programs. Subsequent newsletters continued to raise more money. Best of all, even creating the first issue required significantly less effort than the Valentine's Day card sale.

◆ We implemented a sponsorship program for the annual dinner. In addition to selling event tickets, we created sponsorship levels at $1,000, $2,500, and $5,000. The first year we got one of each! We ended up with $8,500 dollars plus thirty new people (three tables) at the dinner that we had never had before. In subsequent years, we were able to build on the initial momentum and solicited and received more and more sponsorships each year.

◆ We added a silent auction to the dinner, which raised almost $10,000. Although this one was a lot of work, it netted almost *five times as much* as the card sale for about the same amount of effort.

◆ We created an individual-giving "brick" campaign where we sold bricks with people's names on them. This also was labor intensive, but instead of netting $2 per box of cards, we netted over $200 per brick.

Implementing these new development strategies was much smarter fundraising than the card sale. For the amount of effort required, they yielded much greater results: more dollars raised, new donors, and increased public awareness.

Do you have any fundraising events that don't earn the amount of money they should for the amount of effort required? I specifically say *fundraising* events, because organizations have lots of other reasons for having events, such as publicity, community awareness, or cultivation. Those types of events aren't fundraising events and shouldn't be expected to raise money.

The Pareto Principle

The Pareto principle, better known as the "80/20 rule," can be applied to many fields. In fundraising, it means that 20 percent of donors give 80 percent of your dollars. In many cases, the top 10 percent of donors alone give an organization 90 percent of its income! Find out what the ratio is for your organization, and pay most attention to those top donors.

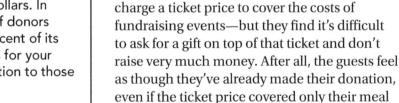

Think carefully about the purpose and format of your fundraising events. Most organizations charge a ticket price to cover the costs of fundraising events—but they find it's difficult to ask for a gift on top of that ticket and don't raise very much money. After all, the guests feel as though they've already made their donation, even if the ticket price covered only their meal and other expenses.

Once you consider revenue versus expenses for your events and appeals, including staff and volunteer time, you might discover some that need cutting. Or perhaps you'll identify ways to make these efforts more efficient and effective.

Fundraising Is a Team Sport

Another aspect of getting ready to raise more money by putting the 50 Asks plan in place is to make sure you have the team you need to succeed. Fundraising should never be the responsibility of a single individual, whether that person is a staff member or a volunteer. In a nonprofit organization, fundraising is everyone's responsibility.

This is so important I'm going to repeat it: Fundraising is *everyone's* responsibility. Your organization needs to take an "all hands on deck" approach to reach your fundraising goal.

We'll talk more about roles and responsibilities later, but for the moment think about all of the ways your organization "touches" donors and prospects—from the person who answers the phone to the volunteer who gives tours. Are these people interacting with prospects and donors in ways that make your funders feel welcome and gives them a sense of ownership in your mission?

Of course, the primary, day-to-day responsibility for fundraising (as in actually making asks) does lie with your organization's leadership. Although your board members should be involved and engaged, your nonprofit's bottom line is primarily the responsibility of your executive director and fundraising staff.

Executive directors should spend 25 to 50 percent of their time raising money. That's right—a quarter to half of an executive director's time should be spent on fundraising, regardless of whether or not an organization has fundraising staff members. And when a fundraising person is hired, the executive director does *not* get to hand off the fundraising responsibilities but remains responsible for coordinating with that person.

Organizations with several people (such as executive director, fundraising staff, and board members) who are actively involved in fundraising are generally the most successful at fundraising, regardless of the economy or the type of organization they're raising money for. Before you get started creating your plan, think about whether or not you have the right team in place. If not, what changes can you make?

The Case for Support—and How to Create a Strong One

Another piece of the fundraising puzzle is a solid case for support. A case for support, or *case statement,* is a written document that conveys the important work of the organization and explains why it deserves financial

---

Train Your Team!

There is no such thing as a "born fundraiser." In fact, most people are at least a bit nervous about asking others for money. Therefore, you need to train your team members for them to be effective in their fundraising role. Fortunately, this is fairly easy to do. For example, you can include fundraising training as part of your annual board retreat as well as at regular board meetings.

You may need to hire an outside facilitator to provide training, or you may have someone in-house who can do it. You will also want to provide fundraising-related professional development opportunities for the executive director and fundraising staff. (There are many low-cost training options, including webinars.) Finally, I strongly encourage you to join your local chapter of the Association of Fundraising Professionals (AFP).

practical tip

Case Statement

A case statement is a written statement about why your organization is important, deserves donations, and needs them now. In other words, it answers the questions: Why this organization, and why now?

---

support. It's important to be able to communicate the mission of your organization passionately and succinctly, both verbally and in writing. The case for support is your fundraising pitch.

In addition to a written case for support, I believe that it's equally important that staff and board members are able to talk passionately about your organization. Although this particular message won't necessarily be consistent throughout the organization, if done right it will be personal, meaningful, and very persuasive. While this might seem easy and obvious, it's actually quite difficult for most people and takes practice.

To practice talking about your case for support at a board meeting or retreat, have participants (board and staff members) think about what attracted them to the organization in the first place and why they continue to be involved. After a few minutes, ask everyone to stand up and pair off. The pairs should tell each other (in two to three minutes) why they're involved, and what they love about the organization. Once they've had a chance to tell their story, switch partners and repeat.

Do this three or four times, or until everyone has spoken to everyone else. With every telling, each story becomes more concise and articulate. Board members learn about each other and why each of them joined. This is a very powerful experience, especially for those who might not feel as connected to the cause. Each participant is now prepared to go out into the community and tell these same stories to friends, neighbors, colleagues and other prospective donors at cocktail parties, in the grocery store, or at work.

This conversational method isn't your formal case for support, but it will definitely get the message across. As you probably know, people give to people, not just to organizations or causes. This personal perspective is extremely powerful in recruiting friends and donors to your organization.

Prospect, Identification, Cultivation, Solicitation, Stewardship

A *prospect* is an individual, foundation, or corporation that you've identified as a potential donor to your organization.

Identification is the first stage of the fundraising cycle. This is the stage during which you figure out who your prospects are.

Cultivation is a process where prospects and organizations get to know one another. In other words, board and staff members educate prospects about the organization and get to know their potential donor. Cultivation takes place over a period of time, and can last from a few months to several years before asking for a gift.

Solicitation is the actual ask. This stage is what most people think of when they hear about fundraising. Solicitation generally lasts for only one moment in time, while the rest of the process is ongoing. Solicitations can happen in person, by mail, by application, or by phone.

Stewardship is the thanking or follow-up stage. It's vitally important to steward donors properly after the gift is made.

Fundraising from Start to Finish

There are four stages of fundraising that apply to all fundraising activities and prospective donors. I'll discuss each stage in detail throughout the coming chapters, but for now, here they are:

1. *Identification.* Who are your prospects or potential donors?

2. *Cultivation.* The "getting to know you" stage, or building a relationship between the organization and prospective donor.

3. *Solicitation.* The "ask" or request for funds. (I like to call this the "moment of truth.")

4. *Stewardship*—follow-up and thank yous.

Executive directors, board members, and development staff must understand the entire fundraising cycle, as each participant has an important role to play at each stage.

I created a pie chart (below) to illustrate my experience with the fundraising cycle. The pie represents the amount of time it takes for an organization to identify a prospect, cultivate the prospect, solicit a gift, and steward the donor—regardless of whether the process takes a month, a year, or more.

When board members and executive directors say they don't want to raise money, most are referring to the ask or the solicitation stage. As this pie chart shows, the solicitation is only one event in a much longer process. Most people are willing to get involved in the identification, cultivation, and stewardship stages.

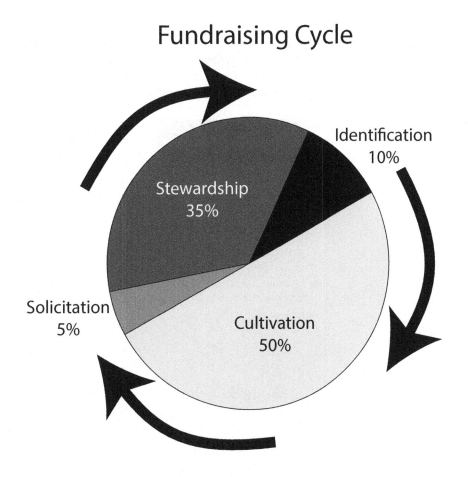

Fundraising Cycle

Identification 10%

Stewardship 35%

Solicitation 5%

Cultivation 50%

Getting to Work: Creating a Baseline and Counting Your Asks

Use the following charts to count the number of asks you're currently making each year. You can use the most recent twelve months, the last fiscal year, or the last calendar year, as long as you're consistent in your comparisons.

Counting Your Asks the *50 Asks in 50 Weeks* Way

Here's how I count to get to fifty asks in fifty weeks:

Bulk Mail Appeal = One Ask

Bulk mail appeals include event invitations, appeal letters, newsletters with business reply envelopes, and emails with clear requests for donations and a reply mechanism (such as a "Donate Now" button). Each bulk mail counts as one ask regardless of whether you're sending it to 50, 500, or 5,000 people.

Individual Request = One Ask

Asking an individual for a specific amount for a specific project or purpose, in person, face-to-face.

Grant Proposal (or Application) = One Ask

This means you have completed the full proposal according to the funder's specific guidelines, not just sent a generic application or letter of inquiry.

Sponsorship Solicitation = One Ask

Sponsorship requests are specific to each prospective sponsor, and not a form letter with the name and address as the only changed information (such letters count as bulk mail). Preferably you have a personal (or business) contact or relationship (or one of your board members does) with the person or company being asked to help personalize the solicitation.

List Current Asks: Foundations/Corporations

Year: 2021 YTD

	Foundation/Corporation Name	Amount Requested/ Amount Received	Due Date
Example	XYZ Foundation	$15,000 Requested/ $10,000 Received	February 15
1	Four Rivers Garden Club		
2	Maryland Heritage Areas Auth.		
3	Maryland State Arts Council		
4	WaWa Foundation		
5	NEH		
6	IMLS		
7	Unity Gardens		
8	SAI		
9	4Imprint		
10			
11			
12			
13			
14			
15			

TOTAL REQUESTED: $ _____

TOTAL RECEIVED: $ _____

TOTAL ASKS: _____9_____

List Current Asks: Individuals (Face-to-Face Solicitations)

Year: _2021 YTD_

	Name	Amount Requested/ Amount Received
Example	Mrs. Donor	$10,000 Requested/$6,500 Received
1	Sue Dodds	
2	Laura Martien	
3		
4		
5		
6		
7		
8		
9		
10		
11		
12		
13		
14		
15		

TOTAL REQUESTED: $ _____ 2

TOTAL RECEIVED: $ _____

List Current Asks: Sponsors

Year: _____

	Sponsor Name Individual or Corporations	Event (Golf or Gala)	Amount Requested/ Amount Received
Example	XYZ Company	Spring Gala	$5,000 Requested/ $5,000 Received
1	Edgewater Liquors		
2	Dowells		
3	Griffins		
4	Langers		
5	Kreter		
6	Kirkpatrick-Howat		
7	Konschnik		
8	Lerch		
9	Gundlach		
10	Integrity ~~correct~~		
11	Sandy Spring Bank ~~correct~~s		
12	Karen Whaley		
13	B		
14			
15			

TOTAL REQUESTED: $ _____ 12

TOTAL RECEIVED: $ _____

List Current Asks: Bulk Solicitations

Year: _2021 YTD_

	Name/Description	Number Mailed/ Number Donors	Total Raised	Date Sent
Example	Spring Appeal	1500 Mailed/ 120 Donors	$4,500	March 10
1	Membership Appeal			
2	Auction Appeal			
3	Bonfire Shirt I			
4	Bonfire Shirt II			
5	Tribute Trees			
6				
7				
8				
9				
10				
11				
12				
13				
14				
15				

TOTAL REQUESTED: $ _____ 4

TOTAL RECEIVED: $ _____

Counting Asks Summary (All Solicitation Types)

Year: _2021 YTD_   _July 2021_

Solicitations	Number of Asks Made	Number of Gifts Made	Notes
100% Board Participation			
Grants	9		
Individuals	2		
Sponsors	12		
Bulk Mail	5		
Other			
TOTAL	~~200~~ 28		

To Recap

◆ You have to ask more often to raise more money.

◆ Diversify your funding base to help ensure financial stability.

◆ Make smart asks. Efficiency and frequency are important, but asks without gifts are meaningless.

◆ A solid case for support is critical to success.

◆ The fundraising cycle has four stages: identification, cultivation, solicitation, and stewardship.

◆ Count your asks to know where you're starting from.

Chapter Two

How to Survive and Thrive: Making Time for Fundraising

IN THIS CHAPTER

- ···→ Getting consensus
- ···→ Setting your priorities
- ···→ Delegating tasks: The role of volunteers, interns, and your board
- ···→ Baby steps are forward steps, too

Starting with the introduction to this book, I've tried to make it very clear that fundraising is a team effort. In this chapter, we're going to talk about just how far that team effort goes. Whether your organization has paid fundraising staff members or not, you won't just need help with fundraising itself. If you're like most folks, you're also going to need help making time to raise money!

If this isn't immediately clear to you, take a moment to consider how you spend a typical day at your organization. How many times do you, for example, answer the phone—whether or not the call is actually for you?

Add that time on the phone to your paperwork load, the number of times someone knocks on your door, any time you're spending doing program work, the hours in staff and committee meetings...you get the picture.

In other words, the point of *50 Asks in 50 Weeks* is *not* to tell you that, to raise more money, you're going to have to add another five to ten hours to your workweek. The *entire* point of this chapter is to make sure that you and your team are able to add fundraising to your schedules without burning out.

With that goal in mind, let's get started.

Getting Consensus

Your first step is to build an organization-wide consensus that raising more money means increasing your capacity to do great work—and therefore, everyone needs to pitch in so that the people tasked with fundraising responsibility can actually get the job done.

Before starting to make concrete plans around raising money, I strongly urge you to hold two meetings: one with your organization's decision-makers (board members and key staff members), and another that includes your entire staff. The agenda for the first meeting should address these four questions:

1. Where is our organization now? What are our strengths and weaknesses, particularly regarding our cash flow?

2. How do we envision our organization, programs, and services—one, five, and even ten years from now?

3. How much money will we need to raise one, five, and ten years from now to make those dreams a reality?

4. What are we, individually and as a group, willing to do to achieve this?

Make your answers as specific as possible. By the end of this meeting, everyone should walk away having made individual, measurable commitments to help your nonprofit achieve its fundraising goals.

In addition to the above agenda, I also strongly encourage you to include a "mission moment" during the course of your meeting to remind everyone present why they care about your organization.

Once your board and lead staff have settled on a step-by-step plan to make it possible to create (or significantly improve) your fundraising program, the next step is to meet with the entire staff and volunteers to get their feedback and buy-in.

Why is this important? Because until you've raised the funds to allow you to hire additional staff, you're going to be asking a lot of your existing staff and volunteers.

For example, you may need to recruit someone to take over some of your nonprofit's tedious, but essential, paperwork. You will need to make time on your calendar to help create and implement your fundraising plan—time when, ideally, you shouldn't be interrupted. Including your existing staff and volunteers in your overall plans from the beginning will ensure they understand that the extra work or inconveniences you're asking from them today will create a stronger, more vibrant, and increasingly stable organization for everyone.

Mission Moment

As the name suggests, a mission moment is a pause you take during important meetings to remind participants why they committed themselves to your nonprofit in the first place.

The mission moment can be many things depending on the type of organization and can include client testimonials, a short video, or staff member story.

If yours is a social service agency, you might ask a client to come in and briefly share how your work has changed (or even saved) the person's life. A local environmental nonprofit might want to show a video of the last river cleanup day. Whatever you choose, the point of the mission moment is to energize your volunteers, to reassure them that your organization is making a difference, and inspire them to do the work ahead.

Setting Your Priorities

There are entire books, courses, and websites dedicated to the topics of priority-setting and time management. Why? Because just as people have different learning styles, the way we "tick" will make them respond better to some time-management systems than others.

This section assumes that you are the person (or one of the main people) who will be in charge of creating and implementing your nonprofit's fundraising plan. To allow yourself the time for fundraising, I'm going to provide you with a few quick suggestions for setting and sticking to your priorities. You'll be able to find and choose the time-management system that works best for you.

Right now, though, I'd like you to take a piece of paper and write out all of the tasks you do in the course of a normal week. Write the tasks out as a list in whichever way works best for you—for example, you could do a Monday through Friday list and write your tasks under each day, or simply write a list of every separate item of work you do. Here is a sample worksheet:

Task	Essential?	Can I Delegate?	Notes
Gratitude Comm.			
Weekly Emails			
Monthly Emails			
Signing Letters			
Grant Proposals			
Grant reporting			
Planning			
Ad buying			
Writing Appeals			
Sending Appeals			
Talking w/ Donors			
Meeting w/ Staff			
Graphic Design			
Website Mgt.			

Prof. Development
Auction/event mgmt.

Now, next to each item, ask yourself and write "yes" or "no" to the following:

1. Is this task essential to my organization's survival?

2. Is there someone else—a staff member, board member, or trusted volunteer—who can take this task over with a minimum of training and/or oversight?

Obviously, any task that is both essential *and* unique to your skills needs to stay on your plate. But if you're like most, you're going to be surprised at just how many inessential things you have taken on, *and* at how many qualified people you have on hand to take some of the essential jobs off your plate.

However, if you find yourself in a position (which can definitely happen in smaller organizations) where you really are the only person who's able to perform the most of your organization's essential tasks, *and* those tasks take up the majority of your day, you have at least two options available:

◆ Recruit new volunteers or board members who can take over a few of the essential tasks

◆ Realize that you'll need to delegate more of the actual asking to others—and find ways to make sure those people are properly trained

If any (or all) of the above is making you nervous, remember—if you followed my advice in the introduction and are working your way through this workbook chapter by chapter, you've already done the work of getting consensus from your staff and board! The people who matter have agreed that it's important to improve your organization's bottom line significantly, *and* they've pledged to take on extra work to help you find the time to make it happen.

Now that you've identified what your priorities should be, let's talk about delegation.

The Art of Delegation

So far in this chapter you've met with all of the key people in your nonprofit and gotten consensus that you want to improve your organization's bottom line. You've identified all of the tasks that get in the way of fundraising. Now it's time to get those tasks out of your way.

Before we start talking specifically about delegation, though, it's important to remember *why* you're doing this. After all, most of us who dedicate our professional lives to nonprofit work do so because we're people who enjoy giving. Sometimes, we're *also* people who have a hard time receiving—including receiving the help we need.

If you're having issues with the idea of delegating some of your work to concentrate on fundraising goals, I invite you to think of delegation this way: you're not just asking for something, *you're giving another person an opportunity* to work with you to further your nonprofit's important mission. In fact, delegating some of your work is very much like asking a prospect to make a gift to your organization.

Of course, delegation doesn't mean giving someone a task and then walking away. It's quite possible you'll need to provide some training (particularly in cases of more complicated or exacting items), and you'll want to schedule regular times to check in to make sure the jobs are getting done. But as you get your helpers in place and functioning smoothly, you'll also be freeing up increasing amounts of time to use for your fifty asks.

The Role of Staff, Interns, and Your Board

While some of what I'm about to say about delegation may seem obvious, I'm including it for two reasons:

1. Just as the majority of nonprofit leaders come into their roles with little or no fundraising training, it's also true that a lot of nonprofit leaders haven't had much (or even any) management training or experience. Instead, they're dedicated people who became involved to help others and (sometimes sooner rather than later) find themselves growing into the role of board member, executive director, or other leadership-level staff.

2. *50 Asks in 50 Weeks* is a step-by-step guide, and creating or improving a fundraising program doesn't happen in a vacuum. This workbook assumes that your plate is already overflowing. So even if you already know all about delegation, it can't hurt to have something to refer to as you go through the process of (perhaps radically) changing the way your nonprofit raises money.

With that in mind, here's a quick primer on choosing the right people to take on some of your nonfundraising workload:

Other staff. Delegating to other staff members has several advantages. Working for your nonprofit is their job, so they have an obvious incentive to help out. They also know your organization and may already have an idea of how best to do the task. However, proper delegation also means doing your best to make sure you're not expecting too much from them.

Interns. On the plus side, interns are fantastic for contained projects—for example, designing your print or online newsletter, or organizing a mailing. But since interns often leave after a semester or two, delegating ongoing tasks to them may mean you find yourself going through the training process a few times a year. Remember, the point of delegation is to save time for fundraising, *not* to spend it on training interns! "Delegating smart" is just as important as "asking smart."

Volunteers. If you're reading this book, I doubt you need me to tell you both the pros and cons of delegating to volunteers. Suffice it to say that the ability and *dependability* of the volunteer you choose for a task need to be in direct proportion to the importance of that task.

Board members. With any luck, you have a board made up of a diverse set of people with a diverse set of talents. If a member of your board is an accountant, for example, perhaps that person would be willing to take over your bill-paying responsibilities (as long as there's no conflict of interest, and all of your checks and balances are in place, of course). Any nonfundraising tasks you delegate to a board member should be in *addition* to that person's assistance with fundraising.

When You Need to Learn More

I've written more on the subject of delegating—particularly as it relates to fundraising—in my

---

> ## Proper Delegation Benefits Everyone
>
> When you delegate a task, you benefit your nonprofit and the people involved with it in at least two important ways:
>
> 1. You give them the opportunity to have an even greater impact on your organization's mission; and
>
> 2. You help them feel more "ownership" of your overall work—and in the case of interns (and perhaps even some of your volunteers) you provide them valuable professional experience.
>
> Proper delegation means everyone wins—you, the people you serve, and the people who take on the new tasks!
>
>

book *Major Gift Fundraising for Small Shops: How to Leverage Your Annual Fund in Only Five Hours per Week.* That's right—just five hours per week!

I bring this up because while you may well need more than five hours a week to boost your current fundraising program up to fifty asks, I *know* you can get there with the right team and by using proper delegation!

Baby Steps Are Progress, Too

The positive thing about creating ambitious plans—like deciding to do *50 Asks in 50 Weeks*—is that the very ambition of the goal is hugely motivating.

The downside, though, is that it can be very easy to be discouraged if a week comes along where you aren't able to make an ask for any reason.

That's one of the reasons this book is called *50 Asks in 50 Weeks*, not *52 Asks in 52 Weeks.* For one thing, I hope you'll be taking a vacation this year! For another, fundraising is just as much a process as it is a destination.

Your organization may well fly through the 50 Asks process, depending on factors such as the state of your current fundraising program and the resources you have on hand right now. Other nonprofits, though, may find themselves increasing from, say, their usual three grants to "just" fifteen asks during their first year working this system—*but that's still a five-fold increase in the number of asks!*

The idea of even going from ten or twenty asks to fifty in a single year is probably unreasonable, so set yourself a reasonable goal based on where you are. Conversely, if you find that you're already making many more than fifty asks, then how many more can you make? Are all of your asks as smart and effective as they could be? If some funders pull back, is your fundraising base diversified?

> ### What's a Reasonable Goal?
>
> Regardless of whether you are currently making ten asks or one hundred, it is your job to ensure that every year, you are increasingly asking for more (both in number of gifts and amount from each ask) and in smarter, more effective ways.
>
> This means that if your current baseline is ten asks, then a more reasonable goal might be fifteen, twenty, or even twenty-five asks. If on the other hand, you are asking one hundred times per year, you may want to look at the quality of those asks. If they're all effective, then strategize about how you can do 110 or 120 moving forward.
>
> **Example**

So while the ultimate goal of this workbook—and *your* ultimate goal—is and should be to make fifty asks in fifty weeks (or more), don't forget to celebrate the milestones you achieve along the way!

You're the Conductor, Not the Orchestra

I want to reiterate something I've mentioned several times so far: whether you're a board member or other volunteer, your nonprofit's executive director, or the director of development, *it isn't your job to make all fifty asks.*

As I've said before, fundraising is a team effort, including all staff members, volunteers, and members of your board. There are many different parts to fundraising, and everyone should be involved in the different steps of the process.

While you—the person who has taken on the responsibility for the overall fundraising plan—may well end up making the majority of the asks yourself, ideally your role will be more like that of an orchestra conductor. It's the conductor's job to make sure all the parts of an orchestra are playing together smoothly. A fundraising program suffers if no one is taking care of a combination of the big picture and the details—ensuring donors are thanked, on one hand, and that donor information is being correctly entered into your database, on the other, to use just one of many examples.

To Recap

◆ Setting priories and delegating tasks will ensure the job gets done.

◆ Lay the foundation before you start (or build up to) a 50 Asks fundraising program.

◆ You may be able to reach fifty asks in fifty weeks right out of the gate, or you may not. Either way, celebrate your milestones along the way.

◆ The person who is responsible for your nonprofit's overall fundraising program doesn't need to make all of the asks and needs help in all areas of the fundraising process.

Chapter Three

Board Members Are Fundraisers Too

IN THIS CHAPTER

- ···➔ Your board is responsible for your nonprofit's financial health

- ···➔ Train your board members to raise funds

- ···➔ What one hundred percent participation is—and how to achieve it

- ···➔ Boosting your board's giving

You know your board members are responsible for the overall health and direction of your nonprofit. It's their job to set policies, hire the executive director, set the mission and vision, and ensure the financial stability of the organization. But did you know that your board members are *also* responsible for fundraising—and for giving themselves?

If you weren't aware of this, don't feel bad. For a whole range of reasons, there are many nonprofit leaders (board and staff alike) who don't know the full extent of a board's responsibilities. Others know what a board should do, but have trouble implementing it.

I've addressed this problem with many organizations over the course of my consulting career. Solving the problem doesn't mean that every single member of every nonprofit board will have the ability or willingness to raise a lot of money. What it *does* mean is that even those board members who can't—or *won't*—ask need to be involved in the fundraising process in a meaningful way.

The fundraising responsibilities of your board—and tactics for helping them shoulder those responsibilities—are the focus of this chapter.

While they love and value their volunteer board members, executive directors and development staff often complain to me that their organization's board members aren't doing their fundraising jobs.

I certainly understand the frustration! However, it's also true that one of the primary *reasons* that board members don't step up to the plate is that we, the staff, haven't adequately prepared them for the job!

To build nonprofit boards that fulfill all of their responsibilities—including fundraising—we must provide prospective and new board members with a comprehensive job description, including appropriate expectations, an orientation session, and ongoing training and support.

Before we can even *consider* whether it's time to ask a board member to step down, our first step must be to make sure each member of our board is properly informed, oriented, and trained.

This is what nonprofit board members, prospective board members, and nonprofit staff members need to know about the role of the board of directors.

Nonprofit boards have two primary responsibilities—governance and fundraising. Governance is generally more popular and includes setting policies and procedures, overseeing investments and the budgeting process, and making sure the organization fulfills its mission.

Governance

Governance: Setting organizational policies, creating the mission and vision, overseeing the budget and investments, and hiring, evaluating, and (if necessary) firing the executive director. In other words, overseeing the big picture.

Contrary to the belief of many board members, boards are *not* responsible for the daily management of their organization. The day-to-day work of a nonprofit is the responsibility of its executive director, not the board. That said, it is true that one of the primary management functions of a nonprofit board is to hire, fire, and evaluate the executive director.

Of course, even organizations that do a great job of educating prospective board members can end up with some who want to take part in governance but at the same time aren't willing to ask for or to give money. Therefore, you may find it useful to remind reluctant board members that there won't *be* an organization to govern unless sufficient funds are raised.

You may find yourself in the position of having one or more board members who love to govern but are unable or unwilling to help in any way with fundraising, including opening

---

Financial Stability

Financial Stability: Helping oversee the budget and investments, in addition to helping with fundraising *and* making a personal gift annually.

---

those doors, making a gift, or even simply helping with thank-you notes. It may be time to have a candid conversation about alternate volunteer opportunities.

Now that we've established that your board members are responsible for helping with your organization's bottom line as well as deciding how the funds are spent, let's talk about their specific responsibilities as *donors and fundraisers.*

Give *and* Get

Have your heard the old expression "give or get"? (By the way, the new expression is give *and* get.) This phrase, however you say it, refers to board members. It means that they need to *give* money and *get* money, or *get* off the board.

Why put this so directly? Because if your board—the people who are the closest to your nonprofit—aren't making donations, why should anyone else? Your board members need to be the first to step up and invest in your organization so others will follow. They should set the tone and lead your organization in this important way.

This diagram represents your nonprofit, with your board and staff as the innermost circle. Donors and supporters are next. Finally, the outermost circle represents the community at large; those who live or work in your community and could be converted into donors or supporters. *When fundraising, always start with the innermost circle and work your way out.*

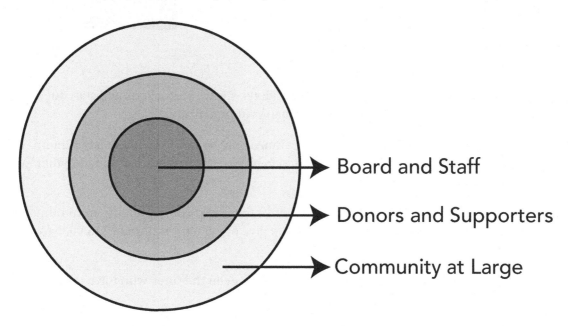

Achieving One Hundred Percent Participation

One hundred percent participation means that everyone on the board writes a personal check. This is essential for your future fundraising success. If board members don't give, why should anyone else?

I mean that question literally. Many foundations, corporations, and savvy individual donors are asking organizations about board giving before making their own decisions. Having 100 percent board participation shows that your entire board is truly committed to the cause.

Board members should be the first people asked to give a donation to your organization each year, and they should be the first to make their annual commitments. It's the job of your board to "kick off" your annual fundraising campaign and to be the first to give when you hold a special campaign.

Here are some questions to ask:

◆ Are all board members giving? If not, why not? Are they giving minimal amounts, or stretching and giving generously?

◆ Have board members been individually asked to make a gift?

◆ Have board members been asked to help fundraise? Have they been given the training, guidance, and tools to be successful?

If you have a nondonating board member who is also a star volunteer, it's time to schedule an appointment with that member and the most appropriate person—the board president, for example. Whoever meets with the board member needs to explain that any gift (no matter how small) will be deeply appreciated and that every board member is expected to give.

I have yet to meet a board member with a job who can't give at least $100. If necessary, allow them to make quarterly or monthly payments of $25 per quarter or $10 per month.

One Hundred Percent Participation

One hundred percent participation refers to how many board members are making financial gifts to your organization. For your board to achieve 100 percent participation, every member must contribute.

When having these admittedly uncomfortable conversations, always be gracious and start out by expressing your appreciation for the member's service to your organization.

In addition to the expectation of 100 percent participation, some boards implement a minimum "give or get" amount. In other words, members are expected to give *or* raise (or any combination thereof) a minimum, preset amount.

While this approach sets a clear expectation, I don't love these sorts of mandatory minimum arrangements. Why? If you require a board member to give or get a minimum of $1,000, two things can happen:

1. All the members who are able will give $1,000—even the ones who have the capacity to give more.

2. Hardworking, loyal board members who don't have the capacity to give or get the full $1,000 will resign.

Instead of mandatory amounts, I like to encourage each member of the boards I work with to make a *stretch gift*. This is a gift that's large for that specific member's own budget. Frequently, this tactic results in a larger total gift from the board than can be achieved with a mandatory minimum gift level—as long as you follow through and ask each board member in person.

Foundation Denies Grant

I once worked with an organization that applied to a foundation that required 100 percent participation from board members. The executive director was honest in telling the foundation that there was one member who didn't give.

The foundation refused to consider a grant unless the nonprofit reached 100 percent participation.

Only after he cost them a grant did the board member fully understand the implications of his actions. He finally wrote a check—and the organization received that grant during the next cycle.

stories from the real world

Easy Methods to Boost Board Giving

Ready for some fun? Let's take a look at some easy methods to boost giving by your board members. This is low-hanging fruit, yours for the asking.

Provide Quarterly or Monthly Payment Plans

Many board members can significantly increase their giving if you provide a monthly or quarterly payment option. For example:

A member who gives $150 annually might be willing to give $50 per quarter. If so, that member will increase the gift by 25 percent (to $200 annually).

A member who gives $500 annually might be willing to give $100 per month, for a total gift of $1,200—increasing the gift by more than 50 percent!

> **Stretch Gift**
>
> A *stretch gift* is a gift (of any amount) that is large, or *a stretch*, for that particular donor's budget. A stretch gift is a contribution that requires serious thinking before giving and is often sufficiently large that the donor will discuss it with a spouse or family member first.
>
>

The key here is to make sure your nonprofit has the capacity to accept credit cards and to charge the cards without bothering the board member each time. This way you don't have to rely on your board members to write checks—*and* you're not in the position of being seen as "nagging" them about their payments. *Don't lose money because you can't collect pledge payments.*

Expect to Be in the Top Three

Ask each board member to create a confidential list of his or her own annual giving, listing the charities or causes and the amounts. This list is for the board member's eyes only. Then tell them that, as board members, they should each be making a "stretch" gift to your organization, meaning that it should be one of the *top three* gifts they make each year.

Provide a Challenge or Matching Gift Opportunity

A board member, individual, or company can provide a *challenge* gift to your organization and structure it so that each board member must participate to receive the gift. For example, a board member could pledge $10,000 if the rest of the board combined collectively gives the same amount.

> **Monthly Giving—It's Not Just for Your Board**
>
> If you haven't created a system that allows *all* of your donors—not just your board—to make monthly credit card gifts, set one up as soon as possible. Your board members aren't the only people who are likely to give more if you make it easy for them to do so!
>
>

Create a Fundraising Competition between Board Members

Encourage your board to come up with new, creative ways to challenge themselves. Give them some examples that have worked in the past. I've coached nonprofits whose boards decided to set an overall board goal, such as $25,000. One member was able to give $10,000. Another was able to give $3,000, and seven gave $1,000 each. The remaining members each gave gifts of around $500 for a total board gift of $25,000. Without the challenge, the board members might not have felt the need to stretch their giving.

> ### Getting into the Top Three
>
> I once lead a board retreat where a member admitted to giving significantly more to her church than to the organization where she served on the board. Instead, she lumped "her" charity with the rest of her giving— about $100 per year to each of ten or so organizations. Once she understood that board members were being asked to make the organization one of their top priorities, she immediately increased her annual gift from $100 per year to $2,000—still not as much as she was giving her church, but significantly more than she was giving to any other charity. And it was a stretch gift for her.
>
>  stories from the real world

Another way to create competition is to have generous board members call the others and let them know what they're giving, and challenge them to match it or give what they can.

Board members must *give and get* to help jump-start your fundraising this year. Once the entire board has given, you can "check off" one (or more, depending on how you count them!) of your fifty asks.

Getting Your Board Involved in Fundraising

In addition to making their own, individual gifts, boards should help the organizations they serve with all four stages of fundraising: identification, cultivation, solicitation, and stewardship. As we discussed in **Chapter One,** most board members say they don't want to fundraise—but what they really mean is that they don't want to ask (or solicit). However, just because someone is afraid to ask doesn't mean they can't be involved in other ways! Following are some ideas to help your board become involved in each stage of the fundraising process.

Motivating Board Members to Identify Prospects

One of the biggest ways that boards can help nonprofits with fundraising is by "opening doors," or introducing their friends, family, and colleagues to the organization, the executive director, and other staff and board members. This includes scheduling individual meetings, bringing them on tours, and bringing friends and family to events and organization functions.

Board Members and Cultivation

Board members can also assist with fundraising by helping to build relationships between prospective donors and the organization—especially the individuals they have introduced to the organization.

There are many types of cultivation activities. Depending on the prospect and the size of the prospective donation, they can happen over months or even years. (We'll talk about this in more detail in **Chapter Seven.**) Here are a few of the most common:

◆ *Schedule a meeting.* Arranging a meeting between the executive director and the prospective donor is a great cultivation tool! The meeting should take place at a location most comfortable and convenient for the prospect. It doesn't need to be in a restaurant, over a meal. If possible, the board member who is connected to the prospective donors should attend the meeting, in addition to the executive director or development director.

◆ *Host a house party.* A house party is generally in the home of a board member, and the purpose of the party is to provide the board member with an opportunity to introduce friends to the organization in a comfortable, group setting. At these events, the host often covers the cost of food and drink, so the expense to the organization is minimal. House parties are effective because they allow the executive director and board members to meet prospects in an informal setting. House parties generally include a brief presentation about the organization with an opportunity for questions and answers.

◆ *Give a tour.* Another great tool for to get board members involved with cultivation is for them to volunteer to go on or lead tours of the organization's facilities—either with their friends and contacts or with others who are interested in a tour.

◆ *Add a personal note.* Board members can add personal notes to newsletters, annual reports, appeal letters, and thank-you notes, as a way to personalize and further cultivate prospects. A note on a newsletter might say something like, "I thought you might be interested in the article on page two" or "Your picture appears on page three, and thanks again for volunteering."

Getting Board Members to Ask

Peer to peer solicitation is the best way to ask someone for a gift. We want board members to solicit gifts because an ask is often seen as being more heartfelt when coming from volunteers who give their own time and money. However, since you know how difficult this part of the process can be, you need to help your board as much as possible. Give members a variety of ways to get involved in asking, and let them choose the method that works best for them:

◆ Writing a personal note on a solicitation (appeal) letter

◆ Asking their company (or another company they do business with) to sponsor your event

◆ Asking a colleague, friend, or neighbor who heads a foundation to consider a grant or gift to your organization

◆ Making a face-to-face ask of someone they have been involved in cultivating

However, sometimes with all the right coaching and training, there are certain board members who will never feel comfortable enough to ask. Encourage those board members to help with fundraising in the other important ways listed in this chapter!

Thanking Is Easy

Once a donor makes a gift it's critical to thank them in many different ways—so they truly feel thanked and understand the importance of their gift. The rule of thumb is to thank donors seven different times before asking for another gift. Helping express your nonprofit's gratitude is a perfect opportunity for board members to get involved. Members can steward donors in the following ways:

◆ Making thank-you calls

◆ Writing or signing thank-you letters

◆ Saying "Thank you!" in person

◆ Sending a thank-you email

◆ Saying "Thank you!" publicly at an event or in a publication

Multiple people can use each of the above methods of expressing gratitude for gifts. For example, both a board member and a staff member can send individual thank-you notes or make phone calls. (We'll talk details about stewardship, including creating stewardship plans that are time- and labor-efficient, in the next chapter.)

Educating Your Board about Fundraising

Most often, fundraising skills will not come easily or naturally to your board members. They (and you!) will need continuing education on the subject. In addition to an annual retreat (where at least half of the agenda is devoted to fundraising), fundraising skills, expectations, and discussions should be regularly integrated into board meetings. Don't expect your board to rise to the challenge after only a half-day of training! They need support, reminders, and encouragement. It's up to the executive director and development staff to help board members become comfortable, successful fundraisers.

Activities to Engage Your Board

As I've discussed in great detail throughout the chapter, your goal is to raise more money by involving your board members in the entire fundraising process. Below are some specific steps to get them involved on an ongoing basis.

On a *monthly* basis, your board members should be:

◆ Advocating for your organization by discussing it with friends, family, and colleagues

◆ Making thank-you calls to donors

◆ Participating in cultivation activities such as forwarding newspaper articles and sending handwritten notes, emails, or other correspondence to prospects

◆ Forwarding emails from the organization to their contact lists

◆ Engaging with the organization on social media by liking posts and commenting

---

Retreat Generates Needed Turnover

I once led a board retreat where we discussed "give and get" in great detail. At the end of the retreat, several of the board members handed checks to the executive director or made financial commitments for the year. Great! They got the message and stepped up to the challenge.

The same night, other board members asked to step off the board and be put in other volunteer positions with the organization. Also, great! They also got the message that they needed to give *and* get. They weren't prepared to make the commitment, so instead they freed up a space for someone else to join.

In addition to generating gifts from a few board members who had not been giving, the retreat also had the positive effect of dealing with an uncomfortable situation. The executive director needed the nongiving members to leave the board, and the members themselves didn't want to offend anyone or admit to shirking their responsibilities by resigning.

By carefully explaining the board's roles and responsibilities that night, we gave them an easy out—and everyone was happier and better off.

 stories from the real world

Board Expectation Form
(Sample)

Name: _____

As a board member, I understand my financial commitment is necessary to ensure the success of this organization.

My company and/or I will participate in the following ways this year:

___ Awards Dinner Sponsorships from ($5,000 - $10,000) $_____

___ Golf Outing ($300/ticket+sponsorship opportunities) $_____

In order to achieve 100% participation by the board, I personally pledge $_____

TOTAL $_____

For my personal gift, I would prefer to make:

___ One payment   ___ Quarterly payments of $_____

___ My company will match my donation (I will submit the matching gift form with my payment(s)).

Please make gift or first pledge payment by March 1, so we can start the year with 100% participation.

As a board member, I agree to serve on one committee this year (please check):

___ Development Committee   ___ Finance Committee

___ Marketing/Public Relations   ___ Nominating Committee

I understand that board meeting attendance is key to the success of the board and the agency and is a requirement for board membership.

_____   _____
Board Member Signature   Date

Thank you very much for your commitment!

On a *yearly* basis, your board members should be:

◆ Participating in cultivation activities, such as hosting a house party for your organization

◆ Personally inviting their contacts to your fundraisers

◆ Bringing friends and colleagues on tours of your organization

◆ Soliciting prospects (making the ask) when appropriate

Exit Strategies and Term Limits

One simple way to achieve a healthy turnover of board members is to institute and enforce term limits. Term limits will help you "ease out" long-serving members who might not understand the direction your organization is heading. You can also institute a board member "review" at the end of each year and ask some tough questions:

◆ Do you (as a board member) feel you were able to serve the organization as well as you could have?

◆ Did you advocate for, give personally, and raise funds for the organization this year?

◆ Do you wish to continue to serve?

Use a board member expectation form (such as the example on the prior page) to help board members renew their commitment annually.

To Recap

◆ Board members must make personal donations to your organization (give) and raise funds for your organization (get).

◆ Board members need training and ongoing education about their roles and responsibilities.

◆ Board members can help with all stages of the fundraising cycle, regardless of whether they're comfortable making asks themselves.

◆ Asking your board to give, and any asks made by your board members, count toward your fifty asks!

Getting Your Board Moving

❑ Create a job description and expectation form for incoming or potential board members.

❑ Plan for fundraising education, training, and discussions throughout the year, including at regular board meetings and at a board retreat.

❑ Develop a formal orientation process for new board members.

❑ Start a thank-you calling program for board members to thank donors.

❑ Ask board members to add personal notes to all mail appeals.

Asking Your Board. *It Counts!*

Asking your board counts as your first ask for the year. Add it to your list of fifty asks at the end of this workbook.

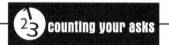

Chapter Four

Donor Retention and the Importance of Stewardship

IN THIS CHAPTER

- ···→ How stewardship affects your bottom line

- ···→ The rule of seven thank yous

- ···→ Treat loyal donors with the gratitude they deserve

- ···→ Time- and cost-effective plans for both small and large donors

If you're reading through *50 Asks in 50 Weeks* chapter by chapter, you may remember the fundraising cycle we discussed at the end of **Chapter One.** In that cycle, stewardship, or building an ongoing relationship with your donors, is listed as the last step of the cycle. So why is there a chapter about stewardship so early in the book?

Even though stewardship is the last stage of the fundraising cycle, to be truly successful, you need to have your stewardship plan in place *before* you either start or boost your fundraising program.

With that in mind, just what is stewardship? Simply put, stewardship is the process by which you turn a first-time donor into a loyal donor—someone who makes at least one gift a year, every year. It is how you express your genuine gratitude and help donors understand exactly how their gift made a difference in the lives of others.

Think of stewardship in the same way you think of building any other relationship. If a friend or colleague does you a favor, for example, you say "Thank you." And then you follow up and get in touch again soon... not just when you need another favor!

How Stewardship Affects your Bottom Line

Before discussing how to create a stewardship plan, let's look at some numbers so you can see just why this step is so essential.

According to the Fundraising Effectiveness Project, donor retention rates hover at around 46 percent and are significantly lower for first-time donors. That means that only 46 percent of donors who make a gift to your organization this year will give again next year.

In fact, what every seasoned fundraiser knows is that it costs *five times as much* to acquire a donor as it does to retain one.

Acquisition vs. Retention

Acquisition refers to the number of new donors you have each year. For example, if an organization acquires one hundred new donors per year out of one thousand total donors, 10 percent of its donor base is comprised of acquisitions.

Retention refers to the number of donors you're able to keep from year to year. What percentage and number of donors are you keeping (or retaining)?

The same article also provides a huge incentive for taking the time to create and implement a proper stewardship program. According to research by Dr. Adrian Sargeant, decreasing your organization's donor attrition rate by just 10 percent *can result in a 200 percent increase in the value of your donor base.* That's because happy, satisfied donors are more likely to *increase* the amount they give over time, more likely to make a planned gift (remember your organization in their will), *and* more likely to ask their friends, family, and colleagues to give.

The Rule of Seven Thank Yous

Believe it or not, I've actually known organizations that didn't thank their donors at all! They were small organizations and believed they didn't have the time or resources. Then they wondered why they struggled with fundraising!

I do understand, at least a bit, where this attitude might come from. After all, time is very tight for small organizations. Most nonprofits are working to fill compelling, important, and frequently urgent needs. Put those factors together and it's easy to see how an overworked staff might believe that it's okay to omit a thank you.

However, the two top reasons donors cite for not making a second gift to a particular organization are:

1.   They didn't feel thanked for the first gift; and

2.   They were never informed about how their contribution was used.

These are the reasons it's extremely important to thank your donors. To ensure that your donors feel thanked, you want to thank your donors early, thank them often, and make sure they are thanked by multiple people within your organization. It's called "The Rule of Seven Thank Yous."

How does the rule work? To keep the process time and cost-efficient, you'll want to tailor your stewardship plan by both the amounts your donors are giving and their longevity (more on that soon). However, the example of an in-person major gift is a good illustration of the process.

If someone gives a major gift in response to an in-person solicitation, you will thank the person right then, of course. That's your first "thank you." Then:

1. The next day, someone from the meeting should call to say thank you again and handle any follow-up details.

2. The executive director or someone who attended the meeting should send a handwritten note card.

3. Once the gift actually arrives, a tax receipt should go out with a personalized note.

4. The gift can also be recognized publically in a newsletter, on your website, or at a special event.

5. In approximately six months, you will want to have another in-person meeting to thank the donor again and report back on how the gift was used.

6. Finally, send a follow-up letter from that meeting to reiterate how the gift was used.

Here are sample ways you can adapt this process to the other ways your organization receives gifts.

Gift by mail. When a gift is received by mail, (for example, in response to an appeal letter), get the tax receipt letter out within one week of receiving the gift. (If you can, shoot for within forty-eight hours.) Depending on the size of the gift, you may want to have your executive director send a handwritten card, your development director send an email, or a board member make a thank-you call. This gift can also be recognized in your newsletter or on your website. After six months, send a follow-up letter to thank the donor again and say how the gift was used.

No, Really—Thank You

Why is it important to express your gratitude so frequently? Look again at the first reason people provide for not making a second gift: they don't *feel* thanked. Yes, you may have sent out a single thank-you note—but the donor may never have opened it. I also guarantee they won't remember that one note a year later, even if they did read it.

The Rule of Seven Thank Yous takes care of this issue by making sure your donors are thanked enough to help them remember how much their gifts mean to you. After all, people give because it makes them feel good—and very little makes someone feel better than knowing they're appreciated!

Gift by email/online/credit card. When a gift arrives online, your system should generate an automated thank-you letter. After that, follow the steps for a gift by mail, depending on the size of the gift. Follow up in six months can also be done via email.

Finally, thank the donor one last time as part of asking for the next gift.

Sample Thank-You Letter for Loyal Donors

Dear John and Mary,

Thank you for your recent gift of $300 to support our afterschool program. Your ongoing and continued commitment to keeping children safe is truly incredible. Thanks to you and other loyal donors like you, the children in our area have a safe, fun place to learn and play after school.

Your gift has helped kids like Joey. Joey is a second grader who attends our program every day after school. Joey lives with his mom in a nearby apartment. Joey's mom works hard to keep a roof over their heads and food on the table. Without the afterschool program, Joey would go home to an empty apartment.

At the afterschool program, thanks to your generosity, Joey gets a healthy snack, surrounded by peers and adults who keep him safe and occupied. After snack, Joey and his friends have thirty minutes of structured games and physical activity. After that, they sit down for homework or reading time. Once they have completed their homework, they are encouraged to participate in art projects or quiet games.

Knowing Joey is safe, fed, and entertained gives his mom peace of mind until she picks him up after work.

On behalf of Joey and his mom, we thank you for your ongoing support and generosity.

If you would like to tour our program or volunteer with the children, please let me know.

Sincerely,

Executive Director

P.S. Enclosed is a thank-you note and picture from Joey.

Treat Loyal Donors with the Gratitude They Deserve

Loyal donors are those who give to your organization year in and year out. These are the people you can depend on to keep your lights on and make your programs possible. But if you don't treat them with the gratitude they deserve, they won't stay loyal for long.

So how can you treat your loyal donors well? With any luck, you already have a workable database tool that can be customized to send out specialized thank-you notes to your loyal donors. (We'll talk more about databases in **Chapter Five**.) Run a report every year to see who has made repeat gifts over longer periods of time and arrange special thanks to them.

Ways to thank these special people will vary by the size of their gifts, but can include:

◆ Special recognition in your print and/or online newsletter to donors who have achieved certain milestones

◆ Recognition by name at an event

◆ Featuring loyal donors (with their permission) in your newsletter, your website, or your social media

Treating your loyal donors with special care helps cement your relationship with them. This isn't just good manners; it also has the potential to affect your bottom line as these donors' income increases or when they consider planned gifts (bequests).

First-time Donors Deserve Special Treatment, Too

As I've mentioned, it costs more to acquire a new donor than to secure a renewal gift from an existing donor. So what are you doing to ensure your first-time donors keep coming back? You should have a "new-donor packet" to send them, letting them know just how much you appreciate their gift. The packet should also outline volunteer opportunities and other ways to get engaged.

Your Board's Role in Donor Stewardship

I've already touched on possible stewardship tasks for your board members (particularly those board members who can't bring themselves to make asks). Specifically, be sure to call on your board to take on tasks like adding handwritten notes to your thank-you form letters, writing their own thank-you notes, or making thank-you calls to donors.

Why is it so important that your board members be involved in stewardship? Just as an ask can mean more to a donor when it comes from a volunteer board member, being thanked by a board member has the same kind of impact. And because one of your highest-level volunteers has made the time to do it, it also sends the message that your organization truly appreciates your donors. Having members of your board assume stewardship roles also frees up *your* time to concentrate on other aspects of development.

Scaling Your Gratitude—Stewardship Plans for All Types of Donors

Thanking your donors early and often is important regardless of the size of the gift. After all, today's $10 donor may well give you a four-, five-, or even six-figure gift in the future.

At the same time, just as you need to "ask smart," it's also important to "thank smart." Invest the majority of your stewardship time and effort in the donors who are *already* giving the largest gifts. With that in mind, use this sample plan to customize your nonprofit's plan for all types of donors.

Sample Stewardship Plan

Donors	Tax Receipt Thank-you Letter	Hand-written Note by Executive Director	Phone Call by Board Member	Follow-up in 6 to 8 months
$100 or Less	Within 1 week	n/a	n/a	n/a
$101 to $500	Within 1 week	Within 2 weeks	Within 2 weeks	Letter or email
$501 to $1,999	Within 1 week	Within 1 week	Within 1 week	Letter with note
$2,000 or more	Within 1 week	Within 1 week	Within 2 days	In person

No matter what kind of donor you're thanking, though, remember that fundraising isn't about the money. Instead, it's about what the money allows you to *do*. As you put together your stewardship materials, make a point of sending a message that's not about the size of the donor's check; instead, focus on the impact of the gift.

Using Your Existing Tools

I've already mentioned this concept elsewhere, but for the good of your bottom line, it's important to reiterate that you don't necessarily have to create a lot of new materials to have a solid stewardship program.

Yes, you'll want to write and send different thank-you letters to account for different gifts and types of donors. But these items in and of themselves will take at most a few days, and not very much money, to put together.

Also, you probably already have several existing communications tools that you can use as part of your stewardship plan: your newsletter; your social media channels; your website; and anything else you already do to communicate with your supporters.

To take one of the examples above, you can add a page or two to your current website to thank major donors, loyal donors, and others. Some organizations even have special pages that share select donors' personal stories of why they are involved.

The main point here is to be creative and to work with what you already have in place as much as possible. After all, your donors want their gifts to be spent on your mission—not on thanking them!

To Recap

◆ Most nonprofits don't retain nearly as many of their first-time donors as they could.

◆ To retain as many of *your* donors as possible, prepare your stewardship plan before starting or increasing your fundraising program.

◆ Use The Rule of Seven Thank Yous to create a stewardship plan that ensures your donors *feel* thanked and *know* how their gifts have been used.

◆ Your board members are vitally important members of your nonprofit's stewardship team.

◆ Scale your stewardship plan to the amount your donors give and use any communications resources you already have to save time and money on stewardship.

Chapter Five

Making Bulk Solicitations Less Bulky

IN THIS CHAPTER

···➔ How and why to start a direct mail program

···➔ About data and databases

···➔ Electronic versus traditional mail

···➔ Creating a bulk mail piece

Believe it or not, there are people who actually read flyers and brochures—particularly ones from organizations they care about. And if you do a good job of creating compelling messages with excellent subject lines, your nonprofit's emails won't necessarily end up in your supporters' spam filters either.

I'm talking, of course, about bulk (also called direct) mail—whether you send it on paper or electronically. Either way (and preferably both), this form of ask remains important and effective. Why? Two important reasons:

◆ Bulk mail is a wonderful way to raise unrestricted dollars as well as attract first-time and lower-level donors.

◆ The database you build to carry out your bulk mail program will ultimately become your portal to the world of individual donors and major gifts.

Who receives your bulk mail? I assume that you have a list of names and contact information for people who are interested in your organization; I *hope* you're keeping that information in an actual database (Microsoft Excel is not a database, by the way).

If this isn't the case, it's time to start. Whether your organization currently has only a few dozen donors or a few hundred, it's important to keep track of your supporters and their donations.

When you are first selecting a database, the most important requirements are that you can easily and accurately input data, and more importantly, get your data back out.

Bulk Solicitations, Bulk Mail, and Direct Mail

Bulk solicitations/bulk mail/direct mail refers to paper or electronic solicitations. "Bulk" simply means that you're asking multiple people (hundreds or thousands or more) for a donation using the same solicitation (appeal letter, invitation, or email).

Many organizations get started by using Microsoft Excel, mistaking it for a database. Excel is Microsoft's spreadsheet program, and it is not designed to function as a database—at least, not one that is up to the task. Access is Microsoft's relational database program.

There are several other free or low-cost databases available to organizations just getting started. If your supporter list is small (fewer than one thousand or so names) it's fine to use Microsoft Access or another free product. Just remember: You get what you pay for. Plan on buying a database program after the first few years.

Building Your List

If you don't already have a list of supporters, start building one by collecting the names and contact information of people who might be interested in your organization. You can ask board and staff members for names of friends and colleagues who they would be willing to invite for a tour or to an event. If you start out asking for names for donations, you won't have very many names on your list.

Once you've gotten your list started, build it by collecting information on everyone who attends your events, volunteers, calls for information, visits your website, or (of course) donates money. Make sure you're capturing the basics:

◆ First and last name and spouse's/partner's first and last name

◆ Mailing address

◆ Email address

◆ Phone number(s) (home, business, cell)

◆ Gift history with your organization—all donations, including ticket sales and other purchases

---

Buying a Database

There are dozens of products available for organizations to choose from, and the choice can be overwhelming. Always ask for recommendations—especially from organizations similar in scope and size.

You can purchase the database outright or take out a subscription with an online database provider. Whichever you choose, understand whether you are buying or "renting" the database software and what the company's support system entails. Prices vary widely as well—from about $1,000 per year to as much as $15,000 or more. Fortunately, as a small nonprofit, your database expenses should be on the lowest end of that scale!

As the sidebar defining "GIGO" implies, the size of your contact list is less important than the quality of the information you have about each person. In addition to making sure that the staff or volunteer who works with your database is trained on using it properly, remember to have someone other than that person spot-check the list regularly. To do so, have someone spend fifteen minutes a month or so "pulling" entries from the database and checking to make sure the information is accurate, complete, and up to date.

> ### GIGO
>
> *GIGO* is an acronym meaning "garbage in, garbage out." It refers to the importance of keeping accurate, up-to-date information in your database. Incorrect, incomplete, or outdated information (garbage) *in* your database will result in misdirected, poorly targeted, ineffective fundraising efforts (more garbage) coming *out* of your shop!
>
>

Reasons to Send Bulk Mail

Bulk mail is the way that most individuals start giving to an organization. Bulk mail is also generally how you increase your base of supporters. That means you can have two different reasons for sending bulk mail: cultivation and solicitation.

In bulk mail, the cultivation process is different. In other types of cultivation, you want a dialogue between prospective donor and the individual representing your organization. In bulk mail, cultivation only goes one way: the prospect learns about the organization. Newsletters (email and/or postal mail) are fantastic bulk-cultivation tools. Others include annual reports, brochures, emailed links to newspaper articles, and volunteer opportunities. When the primary purpose of your mail is cultivation, you should keep any solicitations to "soft" asks.

It's also great to do solicitation through bulk mail because that's the way that most individuals begin giving to organizations. By replying with a check or clicking through to give online, individuals tell you that they care about your cause. This makes them strong prospects for larger annual giving.

So how do you go about creating a bulk mail program? First, you have to write the piece.

Writing the Solicitation

Your bulk mail correspondence—whether traditional or electronic—should always tell a compelling story. Use quotes and photos, and explain how your supporters' donations are being used. To be considered as part of your fifty asks, a mailing must also directly ask for, and provide an easy method for sending, a gift to your organization, such as a reply envelope or "Donate Now" button.

> ### Soft Ask vs. Hard Ask
>
> A *soft ask* is an indirect request for donations. For example, a reply envelope included in your newsletter. The main point of the newsletter is cultivation—providing information to your supporters.
>
> A *hard ask* is a direct solicitation. For example, in an appeal letter, the entire purpose of the mailing is to ask for contributions.
>
>

Send appeal letters multiple times a year. If you can't do that yet, send at least one a year, in November, in time for year-end/holiday giving. Your letters should be well written, with no grammatical errors or typos.

Remember your case for support from **Chapter One?** Appeal letters are one of the places you use it. Also, always include a success story from the past year—the more personal the story, the more effective it will be. Again, when appropriate, use quotes from clients and photos.

Since newsletters are a crucial part of any bulk mail program, let's take a look at specific tips for writing them.

Print (Traditional) Newsletters

Your print newsletters should include:

◆ Photos. Many people look at newsletters for the photos and never read a word, so make sure your photos are clear, plentiful, and tell a compelling story. Make sure each photo clearly shows each individual's smiling face.

◆ Success stories.

◆ Organizational updates, including staff and programmatic changes.

◆ Fundraising. A newsletter should include some regular sections on giving such as asking for annual gifts, explaining planned gifts, or telling the story of a donor and the donor's gift to your organization.

Electronic Newsletters

Although you can send your print newsletter by email as a downloadable PDF file, e-newsletters are different from traditionally printed newsletters because we read differently online than we do in print. And, although there are exceptions to this rule, the higher people are on the economic ladder, the more likely they are to be active Internet users regardless of their age.

Ideally, e-newsletters should be *shorter* than the print version. In fact, it should be possible to see the entire thing on a single screen with links to full stories. Always include a way to donate to your organization with a "Donate Now" button.

Establishing a Bulk Mailing Calendar

I encourage you to send mail (a combination of email and traditional mail) as often as you can afford to. But putting together quality mailings takes time and money! If you follow this chapter's guidelines, you won't be able to exceed a reasonable threshold.

An example of a year of mailings might include:

◆ One year-end appeal and one spring appeal (postal mail).

◆ Email solicitations in October, December, and May (three per year)

◆ Email newsletters (monthly if you keep them short)

◆ Two newsletters (spring and fall) with business reply envelopes.

◆ Two event invitations.

Create a bulk mail calendar (sample found at the end of this chapter) and you'll be reaching out to your supporters about once or twice per month.

Donors Anonymous

I once received a very unusual appeal via postal mail. The reply card had space for how much I wanted to give and for my credit card information, but *didn't* include space for my name, address, or any other contact information! I can't imagine what the charity did after receiving credit card donations without knowing who they were from! I'm sure this was an oversight, but it was a *huge* mistake.

Why a mix of electronic and postal mail? As you know, it's important to connect with your supporters using the tools that *they* are most comfortable with. Some look at every flyer; some only rely on their inbox. Although you may feel more comfortable sticking with your print program, email is just as important as traditional mail because it reaches a wide audience for a fraction of the cost.

Why reach out so frequently? Studies have found that donors who have given the most recently are the most likely to give again. To put it another way, if one of your annual donors skips a year, that donor is less likely to give in subsequent years. Similarly, those who have given to you in the last six months are *more* likely to give than those who haven't given in a year. To keep your giving program healthy, reach out often so that your supporters don't become lapsed donors!

Here's another reason to send mail more frequently: I know that *I'm* guilty of letting my mail pile up, even mail from organizations I care about. Sometimes it takes two, or even three, envelopes before I actually sit down and write a check. A regular bulk mail calendar solves these problems.

Lapsed Donors

Lapsed donors, or former donors, are donors who haven't made a gift in the last twelve months.

Getting Started with Email Solicitation

If you haven't yet started an email program, it may take some time for the people on your list to get used to being asked for gifts, and giving them, online. When planning your direct mail strategy for the year, then, be sure to mention your new email program in your postal materials as well as interspersing emails with postal mailings.

Once you've gotten your system set up, though, sending emails to your list should be a relatively easy and inexpensive process. Email is a great way to keep in touch with donors and prospects and keep them updated about your organization. All it takes is a few moments, for example, to send your supporters a link to news articles about your work!

Just because sending email is easy, though, doesn't mean you should be doing it all the time. People are inundated with email these days, so make sure to stick to your calendar and keep your e-blasts short and valuable.

A Quick Note on Online Giving

We'll discuss the role of online giving in depth in the next chapter. In the meantime, the important thing to note right now is that if your organization doesn't have an up-to-date, interactive website, you're seriously behind the times! Savvy donors are researching organizations before they give, and the place they start their search is online and at your website.

If you don't have a comprehensive website that includes (at least) a bit about your history and mission; contact information; success stories; and instructions for giving, prospects who look you up online won't feel confident about you.

Donors aren't stopping at online research—they're also using the Internet to give both more, and larger, gifts every year. As I mentioned when talking about board members' gifts, it's crucial that your organization implement an automatic system for processing credit card donations and make sure that it can accept donations through your website. In addition to accepting donations, your website should also allow visitors to sign up for volunteer opportunities and for your mailing list.

Business Reply Envelopes

If you're creating your first BRE or reply card insert, collect others from several organizations and use the components of the ones you like best. Remember to check with your bookkeeper and data entry staff member to review the data requested on your BRE to make sure you're capturing what's necessary in a format that makes sense. Multiple sets of eyes are always better when reviewing a mailing.

> ### Counting Your Asks
>
> Use the tables at the end of this chapter to count the number of times per year you plan to be in touch with your supporters through traditional and electronic bulk mail. Sending a bulk solicitation once a month is a great goal. Intersperse appeals, newsletters, invitations, and electronic mail evenly throughout the year.
>
>  counting your asks

Tracking Success

There are many ways to track the success of your bulk solicitations. You can add codes to business reply envelopes. (For instance, an appeal sent out in October 2015 could be coded Fall-15.) The codes will let you know which gift came from which appeal.

Track the number of people you mailed to for each solicitation, how many responded, the total amount given, the average gift size for that solicitation, and the high and low gift amounts.

Compare each appeal with the same appeal over subsequent years to know if your donations are increasing or decreasing. Track the number of returning donors, lapsed donors, LYBUNTS (Last Year But Not This Year) and SYBUNTS (Some Year But Not This Year).

Making Bulk Solicitations Successful

Every piece of correspondence you send should make it easy for your supporters to make a gift. Be sure to include a business reply envelope (BRE) *and* instructions for giving online in your postal mailings. When sending email, always include a link to accept credit card information.

Whenever possible, letters should be personalized—addressed to the recipient, not "Dear Friend."

Have board members, staff, and volunteers take the time to write personal notes on as many letters as possible and certainly to all past donors. The more personal the note, the better.

First class (live) stamps on outgoing letters are highly recommended; they make the mailing look less like bulk mail. It is NOT necessary to put stamps on BREs. However, if you can segment your list, add first class stamps to the BREs you send to your highest donors.

Just as you do with your board members, give all of your donors the option to pay in monthly installments on their credit card. This is a great way for a $10 donor to become a $120 donor.

Ask returning donors for larger gifts by including specific ask amounts in your letter whenever possible.

 practical tip

Use this chart to track and compare the success of your appeals. You'll want to create a similar chart tracking the same appeal over multiple years as well.

Solicitation Name/Date	Number Mailed	Number Donors	Total Gifts	Average Gift	High/Low Gift
Example	2,000	180	$11,000	$61	$900/$10
Update email Feb. 20xx					
Spring Appeal March 20xx					
Spring Newsletter April 20xx					
Gala Invitation May 20xx					
Electronic Mini-Newsletter June 20xx					

Fill in this chart with the name of each solicitation and mail dates for each month. Not every box in the chart needs to be filled in.

Month	Appeal	Newsletter	Invitation	Email
Example	Spring	Gala Invite	Appeal	March 30
January				
February				
March				
April				
May				
June				

July				
August				
September				
October				
November				
December				

To Recap

◆ If you don't have a bulk solicitation program, it's time to start one.

◆ Keep accurate track of all donor information in a donor database.

◆ Mail and email as frequently as possible to keep in touch with donors and prospects.

◆ Board members can help with bulk solicitations in many ways, including sending solicitations to their contacts, adding personal notes to solicitations, making thank-you calls, and more.

◆ Track your success.

Chapter Six

The Role of Online Giving

IN THIS CHAPTER

- ---→ The facts about online giving today

- ---→ Your website is a fundraising tool—use it that way

- ---→ Taking it to the (virtual) streets: "Giving Tuesday" and crowdsourcing basics

It's almost impossible to open the business section of the paper, or your favorite magazine about the nonprofit sector, without coming across at least one article on a topic that didn't exist (at least, not as we know it today) before 1991—the Internet. If you're like most of us, you're probably using the Internet to read the articles.

We all know how much the Internet has changed daily life, from how we get our news to the way we research what to buy. Now it's changing fundraising by providing people with more and easier ways to give—and giving nonprofits more ways to research, cultivate, and reach out to donors.

However, it's important to remember that the Internet hasn't changed the fundamental principle of successful fundraising: Raising money, whether in person or online, is all about building relationships.

With that in mind, let's take a look at the state of online giving today and see what our industry needs to do to be prepared for tomorrow.

Facts and Figures about Online Giving

According to the latest statistics, most nonprofit organizations today receive about 10 percent of their income in the form of online gifts.

I can almost hear your reaction. "Only 10 percent? Why, then, are we even talking about this?" It's a reaction I understand, particularly given how much emphasis I placed on "asking smart" in **Chapter One.**

But here are some other important—and encouraging—figures:

◆ Online giving has grown year after year over the last ten years.

◆ Not only are more people giving online—they're giving larger gifts.

◆ Major gifts are also moving online, albeit slowly. Still, according to an article about online fundraising in the May 18, 2014, issue of the *Chronicle of Philanthropy*, the largest single online gift in 2013 was $1 million, with five additional organizations reporting online gifts of over $100,000.

While your organization will probably not be seeing a six- or seven-figure online gift for quite some time, the fact remains that taking the time to create and manage at least one online giving campaign as part of your fifty asks meets the "asking smart" criteria in a number of ways:

Like bulk mail and email, a strong online campaign is a tool your organization can use to identify and begin collecting information on donors—in other words, everyone who makes an online gift. And unlike bulk mail (and some email programs), your costs are the same whether you reach one hundred people or ten thousand.

Using the Internet, even the smallest shop can reach out to and solicit gifts from people throughout the United States. (Remember, you may need to register in states you are soliciting in—including by email and through the Internet.)

Approximately 75 percent of donors research nonprofits online. (And the higher the income level, the more likely the prospects are to be Internet savvy.)

Investing some of your time and resources in online fundraising today will prepare your organization for a future where a much larger portion of your gifts will come via online channels—possibly even major gifts.

Online Fundraising

Online fundraising is used in this book to talk about any and all solicitations you make online, from the "donate now" button on your website to asks made via Facebook, your blog, or other Internet-based channels. Email appeals, which we covered in the previous chapter, are also a form of online fundraising.

Your Website Is a Fundraising Tool—Use It That Way

In today's world, every nonprofit organization needs a website—and not just any site thrown together by an intern! A well-designed, comprehensive site will do several things for your small organization:

◆ Help prospects—both donors and volunteers—find you. Part of creating a well-designed website involves search engine optimization, or SEO. Without going into detail, an "SEO-optimized" site is easier to find on search engines than a website that hasn't been designed with SEO in mind. In other words, you want to make it easy for people who care about your specific cause to find you when they search for related charities on Google or another search engine. SEO is what makes that possible.

◆ Act as your online "ambassador" in much the same way that your board and staff do when interacting with prospects in person. Your website is the first chance you get to impress an untold number of prospects. Make it count!

◆ Build credibility with prospects. In addition to telling the story of your organization, your website can build credibility with prospects in a number of ways, from its professional look and feel to a page that details your finances.

◆ Increase your list. Be sure to collect names and contact information (probably just an email address) from visitors to your site. Offer to give them something in return, such as offering a free ebook on a topic of interest. (For example, an environmental nonprofit might offer an ebook on the best ways to insulate your home.)

◆ Start the cultivation process. You can collect information from the people who visit your website in several ways and ask them to volunteer, such as asking them to sign an online petition or sign up for a cleanup day.

◆ Make giving a variety of gifts easy. A website can have a dedicated page with an online gift form and a way to join your monthly giving club. It could also have a page that explains how to make a planned gift to your organization. In short, you can give prospects everything they need to know to make a contribution.

◆ Provide you with an easy way to thank donors. Consider listing major donors on a special page.

So how can you be sure *your* website does all of the above? This is yet another topic that's large enough for its own book. The main thing you need to remember from this chapter is to bring in a professional to make sure your website is helping, not hurting, your nonprofit's reputation and bottom line.

Today's Social Media: Blogs, Facebook, and Beyond

Let's start with a few questions: why have a blog? After all, isn't everyone on Facebook and Twitter these days? Why not just focus all of our efforts there?

You might just choose to go that route depending on the resources and expertise you have on hand. However, if you *can* afford to maintain a blog at even two posts a month, those posts will both help your nonprofit's search engine rankings and give your prospects an easy way to follow the progress of your work.

> **Can I Do It on My Phone?**
>
> As a busy professional, you probably rely on your smartphone to check your email, navigate to a new place, or even make restaurant reservations. In many ways, they've replaced the desktop (or laptop) computer. That's why it's so important your website (and any electronic correspondence) be optimized for phone screens, not just computer screens. Having a clear, navigable mobile site may make the difference between an appeal that gets a response and one that doesn't.
>
>

If you do choose to do a blog, the important things to remember are to keep most of your posts short (about five hundred words), use lots of compelling pictures, and tell the most personal stories possible.

As for Facebook and Twitter, I have one word for you: Yes. As in yes, it's a very good idea for you to create and use at least one, and preferably both, of these free online tools. Whichever one you choose (or if you choose both), here are some quick guidelines to help you increase your online following—which in turn can lead to more followers and supporters:

◆ Don't limit your posts to asks, or even to news that's focused on your organization. Related news that informs or makes readers laugh will keep them paying attention to your posts.

◆ When you *do* talk about your nonprofit, focus on the impact you're having. The most recent research on the millennial generation shows that this cohort, in particular, doesn't care that much about organizations—they care about having an impact.

◆ Track your results monthly to see what kinds of posts are being read, "liked," and shared. Refine your messages accordingly.

Although it has not yet been determined that social media is generating funds for organizations, both these tools are increasingly important aspects of donor cultivation.

Taking It to the (Virtual) Streets: Giving Tuesday and Crowdsourcing Basics

If you live in the United States, you know about Black Friday. You've probably done a bit of holiday shopping from your desk at work on Cyber Monday. And unless you personally boycott the news during the holiday season, you have at least heard about #GivingTuesday, a movement begun in 2012 to combat the commercialization of the holiday season and encourage people to give back to their communities.

As you may have guessed from its name, Giving Tuesday takes place on the first Tuesday after Thanksgiving in the United States. In 2016, the fourth Giving Tuesday was a huge success: Over $116 million was raised in one day from over seven hundred thousand donors who gave over one million gifts.

I strongly suggest that you consider making a Giving Tuesday campaign one of your asks. For more information, visit *givingtuesday.org*.

Giving Tuesday is just one example of *crowdsourcing* or *crowdfunding*, which is basically a bulk appeal campaign conducted through the Internet. There are several online services that help nonprofits conduct crowdfunding efforts. Each of them has different rules (what you can and cannot raise money for) and different rates and fees.

Regardless of which crowdfunding platform you use, here are some important tips to make sure your campaign is a success:

◆ Make your campaign for a specific achievement (not unrestricted funds) with a set deadline.

> **Getting Started Online**
>
> ◆ Get professional help, whether volunteer or paid, to either create or revise a complete website for your nonprofit.
>
> ◆ Create social media accounts on Facebook, Twitter, or both. (A YouTube page is also a good idea if you're ready to post well-made videos.)
>
> ◆ Research, choose a platform for, and hold one crowdfunding campaign as one of your fifty asks in the next year.
>
>

◆ Publicize your campaign on your website, blog, social media channels *and* your traditional venues.

◆ If at all possible, promote your campaign with videos. On the Internet, videos tell your story much better than static text. If you don't have the resources to produce a professional-looking video, be sure to use lots of compelling photos.

◆ Post frequent updates that focus on how close you are to achieving the purpose of your fundraising, not just on how close you are to achieving your goal.

Tomorrow Is Here

Even if you're not quite ready to completely dive into the digital world right now, the fact is that you do have to get started if you want your nonprofit to thrive. Seventy-five percent of donors are already researching nonprofits online before deciding where to make their gifts.

Also, millennials have grown up using online tools for everything from researching school papers to talking with friends to—yes—giving to charities. However, don't expect this group to do everything on your website. Though millennials may learn about an organization through its website, they rely on connecting with the organization's social networks for ongoing news. The report recommends that, to convert millennials, your organization needs to integrate its website with a strong social media presence, and make it easy to travel from one to the other.

We have chosen nonprofit careers because we want to be the change we want to see in the world. Today's technology and the social changes it has engendered just means that we need to be that change in our fundraising efforts as well.

To Recap

◆ Many nonprofits are seeing a growth in their online giving.

◆ Your website is an important tool for fundraising.

◆ #GivingTuesday is a fundraising campaign you may want to consider for one of your fifty asks.

◆ Millennials are giving more and more online. As the newest generation of donors, it is important to pay attention to their giving styles.

Chapter Seven

Getting Started with Major Gifts

IN THIS CHAPTER

- ···→ How to identify what constitutes a major gift

- ···→ Identifying and cultivating prospects

- ···→ The key to major donor solicitation: the ask meeting

- ···→ Planned giving—testamentary gifts and beyond

Major gift solicitation is a large subject; my last book concentrated on this aspect of fundraising alone! I wrote that book because, in my experience, major gift solicitation is the weakest link in many small fundraising programs. I think the problem comes down to two factors:

- ◆ Fear of asking for money

- ◆ Not knowing where to find the time to do the work involved

If your nonprofit is suffering from either of the above, don't worry. For one thing, you're not alone. For another, these problems are easily solvable. If you haven't read **Chapter Two** to learn how to make time for fundraising, this would be a good time. As for fear of asking for money, we'll cover ways to overcome that issue in this chapter.

But first, let's answer this: why do you need to include major gift solicitations as part of your fifty asks program? The answer is simple. Remember the Pareto principle from **Chapter Two?** Applied to fundraising, it means that nonprofits will receive approximately 80 percent of their funding from just 20 percent of their donors. In my experience, those figures can be closer to 90 percent and 10 percent!

Individuals Matter

If you think you can count on foundations and corporations to be that top 20 percent of donors you're leaving a substantial amount of money on the table. *The vast majority of nonprofit gifts—71 percent in 2015, according to* Giving USA *—come from individual donors.* Not only that, but a further 9 percent of gifts came from individual donors in the form of bequests. In comparison, foundations accounted for just 15 percent of the total. And corporations? A mere 5 percent.

However, those top donors generally don't come forward and make four-, five-, or six-figure gifts out of the blue. In most cases, the only way to make the Pareto principle work for your organization is to find, cultivate, steward, *and ask* them for those larger gifts.

Convinced? Great! Let's get started.

Identifying What Constitutes a 'Major' Gift

Before you can start a major gift program, you must first define what constitutes a major gift for your nonprofit.

Major gift solicitation is a one-on-one process, involving intensive cultivation and stewardship. It can take a year or sometimes more before you ask for and receive a gift. Your time is valuable, and should be spent where it will make the biggest difference for your organization.

Also, by designating your nonprofit's major gift levels ahead of time, you can also create your stewardship plan for major donors and decide what specific types of recognition will follow each type of major gift. (See **Chapter Four** for more on stewardship.)

With all that in mind, how large does a donation have to be to be considered a "major" gift?

The answer is a lot easier than you might think: it depends on the organization. If yours is a very small or very new shop with only small donors, a $500 check might constitute a major gift for your nonprofit—and there's nothing wrong with that!

On the other end of the scale are the very large, very old institutions like universities and hospitals, for whom a major gift may *start* at seven figures.

So how do you figure out what constitutes a major gift for *your* organization? The answer lies in your database.

Major Gift

What is a *major gift*? The answer varies widely depending on your donor base, which is often related to the age and size of any given nonprofit. Some organizations consider hundred-dollar donations to be major gifts— for others, major gifts are seven figures and more.

The term "major gift" can also apply to individuals. A major gift for one person might not be a major gift for someone else. For example, some donors will consider $2,000 to be a major gift, while others can give ten times that much without blinking.

definition

We discussed databases at length in **Chapter Five.** If you haven't read that section or if you haven't put your donor information together into a workable database, do it now. Once you have the required information together, including each donor's all-important history with your nonprofit, here are the steps to identify what constitutes a major gift:

Run a report identifying your top ten individual donors from the past year. Look at their individual, cumulative totals—that is, the sum of each of their gifts for the year. Do these fall into a fairly narrow range, or are there one or two outliers who have given far more than anyone else? Once you have these figures, have a meeting with your upper-level staff and board and use the results of your search to determine your nonprofit's major gift levels. As a general guideline, you should set your major gift levels at an amount within the range of the *total yearly gift range* of your top ten donors.

Run a report to identify your top 10 percent of donors. What is the range of giving levels within that group?

Another way to determine your major gift levels (particularly if you're still working to create a solid list of donors) is to think about the most recent check you received that was cause for celebration in your office. Does a check for $500 make you want to throw a party, or does it take a gift of $5,000 or more before you break out the funny hats?

Whatever amount makes you want to jump up and down—*that* is a major gift to your organization.

After completing the above list, you'll have a rough idea of how much a major gift is at your organization. If you already have a few individuals who are making cumulative gifts close to that range, you also have your first few major gift prospects. However, to include major gifts as a solid part of your 50 Asks plan, you want to start with a list of ten to twenty major gift prospects.

Don't have that many? Not to worry—next we're going to talk about how to identify the rest of your major donor prospects.

Identifying Major Donor Prospects

The first step in identifying the rest of your major donor prospects is to turn to your database once again. This time, though, you'll be searching for your highest and most loyal donors.

Your Highest Donors

High donors can be defined in many ways, so run all of the following reports to make sure you're not leaving anyone out:

> ❑ The *largest single gifts* given in a
> particular year (generally the most recent year or the last 18 months)
>
> ❑ The highest *cumulative total giving for that year*
>
> ❑ *Lifetime* high giving

> **Starting a Major Gift Program**
>
> Before identifying major gift prospects and starting the cultivation process:
>
> ❑ Determine the amount that constitutes a major gift for your nonprofit.
>
> ❑ Create your major donor stewardship plan by filling in the stewardship chart in **Chapter Four**.
>
> ❑ Create all major donor materials, including your solicitation packet (case for support, program budget, if appropriate and necessary) and thank-you letters.
>
>  to-do lists

Looking for cumulative giving in a year is important because you might have one donor who gives $1,000 every December and another who gives $100 monthly, or $1,200 a year. The second larger donor won't show up if you limit your search to single gifts!

When running these reports, remember to include all donations, including event income from individual donors.

Your Most Loyal Donors

Look for donors who are loyal givers, regardless of the amount. If you have the data, look back for individuals who have given every year (or most years) for five, ten, or more years—even if they've only given $25 per year. (You don't want to leave donors out if they accidentally skipped one year.) If they have the capacity, these are your most likely candidates for major gifts; they're clearly committed to your organization. Even if they can't make a major gift now, with the right cultivation, they may do so later.

Keep in mind these additional important points about loyal donors:

◆ As we discussed in **Chapter Four,** donor *acquisition* and *retention* is a major issue for most nonprofits. Therefore, you should know your loyal supporters and treat them like VIP's, because you want them returning year after year.

◆ If you don't already know these people, you should find out who they are, why they're so loyal, and if they're interested in getting more involved with your organization. If they give a little without any attention from you, they might give significantly more with some cultivation.

Identifying Major Donors Without a Database

In **Chapter Three** we discussed ways to get your board members involved in fundraising. One of the options I suggest—particularly in the case of members who simply cannot or will not ask for gifts—is to ask your board to identify people in their social and/or professional circles who are likely to have both the inclination and capacity to give. This is the best way to either create your "starter list" in the absence of an existing database or to build your list.

Once you've generated your lists you may find you have more than you need. If so, great work! Now, select the top twenty individuals who you believe to have the *capacity* and *inclination* to make a major gift. Don't choose these names in a vacuum—in addition to soliciting your board to suggest prospects, ask them to look over the list.

You can use a basic rating system to determine their capacity and inclination to the best of your ability.

Capacity Rating for Gift Size:

> 1 = $100,000 +
>
> 2 = $10,000 - $99,999
>
> 3 = $1,000 - $9,999
>
> 4 = Under $1,000

Inclination & Capacity
Inclination means that individuals are philanthropically minded, and have an interest in your organization or cause.
Capacity means that individuals have the means (or ability) to make a major gift.

Give individuals on your list a rating based on what you believe their ability to make a gift is. For example, if you know Sue Smith lives in a certain house and has a certain occupation, then you believe she might be able to give a gift of $20,000. She would be rated "2" for capacity.

You can find publicly available information online to help you determine each prospect's capacity rating using Google (for news articles) and sites like LinkedIn (to learn a prospect's profession) and Zillow (to get an idea of the value of their home).

Inclination Rating:

> A = Very Engaged/Interested
>
> B = Moderately Engaged/Interested
>
> C = Mildly Interested (Not Engaged)
>
> D = Interest Unknown

All board members and active volunteers would be given an "A" rating, and so on.

Anyone who is given a rating of "A1" would be on your top prospect list. If you don't have any, then start with "A2's" for your top prospect list.

After you've narrowed your lists to the top twenty, your goal should be to cultivate actively and solicit them this year as part of your 50 Asks plan. I'm having you start with a list of twenty names because not everyone on that initial list will have both capacity *and* inclination or ultimately make a gift. Starting with a larger list ensures that you will have people left after weeding out those who don't.

See my book *Major Gift Fundraising for Small Shops: How to Leverage Your Annual Fund in Only Five Hours Per Week* for a much more in-depth discussion.

Individual Prospects

List your individual prospects for the year. Post this list above your desk and review it daily. Treat these individuals like VIPs.

	Name	Contact Info Phone/Email	Relationship to Organization	Ask Amount	Ask Date
Example	Ms. Smith	(123) 456-7890 smith@aol.com	Friend of Board President	$2,500	June
1.					
2.					
3.					
4.					
5.					
6.					
7.					
8.					
9.					
10.					

Cultivating Major Donors

Each person on your Top 20 list should have an individualized cultivation plan. (See the sample plan in this chapter.) We've already touched on the subject of cultivation in **Chapter Five.** To review: Cultivation is the process of getting to know your donors—and letting *them* get to know *you.* Cultivation can take many forms, but when dealing with major gift prospects, it is ultimately about building relationships between prospective major donors and the leaders (executive director and board members) of your organization. In this context, building relationships means learning what these individuals are passionate about and gaining an understanding of what motivates them to give.

In other words, a large part of cultivating major donors is listening to them. One of the most common mistakes made by executive directors, development directors, and board members is that they're so eager to talk about the organization that they forget to listen. Listening and *hearing* the person you're cultivating is an important part of the process that fundraisers often miss.

Getting to Know Donors

Major donor prospects can be divided into two categories: Those you already know and those you don't. Obviously, it's generally easier to arrange meetings with people you know and to get them involved in your organization. However, it is still important to meet individually with those you know well, such as board members who you may frequently see in group settings (such as board meetings) but not have much contact with on an individual basis.

The trickier part is developing relationships with individuals you don't know. It's often both helpful and necessary for a board member to make an introduction. A board member can introduce someone to your organization by:

◆ Calling to ask the individual to take a meeting with the executive director

◆ Inviting the individual to take a tour of your program

◆ Inviting the individual to an event, either as a guest or as a sponsor/ticket buyer

◆ Inviting the individual to a house party at the home of a board member or other volunteer

There might be some people you found from your data search who no one knows. Although it might be harder to get your foot in the door with these people, they should be receptive because they've already shown their interest by giving to your nonprofit. To make contact with someone new:

1. Send a letter of introduction to the individual (a precall letter). First, thank the person for the previous support, and second, state that you're interested in meeting and will be calling within a week to schedule a meeting.

2. Follow up on your letter within the designated time frame and call. If you get a machine, leave a message letting the person know that you would like to schedule a time to get together to thank them in person, but also to ask for advice.

3. When you reach the donor, express appreciation for past support. Tell the person that you would also like to ask for some advice, and learn why the donor cares about your work. Since this is a cultivation visit, you can honestly say that you *won't* ask the person for money. (Don't say that you will *never* ask for money; just that you won't ask on this visit. This is a visit for you to get to know one another.)

Who Should Meet with the Prospect?

Ideally, a first meeting should include someone the prospect knows, such as a member of your board or the executive director. Meetings should include two people from your organization—for example, your executive director and a board member. When the executive director or board member is unable or unwilling to meet with prospects, the development director can initiate and attend the meeting.

Where Should You Meet a Prospect?

Over the course of building a relationship, you will most likely meet with a prospect on many occasions and in many different locations. The first meeting, though, should take place wherever prospects are most comfortable. You can do this by offering to meet at their convenience and letting them know that you would be happy to come to them and meet them at their home or office.

> **Skip Lunch**
>
> You don't have to take prospects out for a meal. For one thing, restaurants are often noisy and can be awkward for a first meeting. Other complications include deciding where to go, how to talk and eat at the same time, and who pays. All of these issues can be avoided by meeting at a home or office. It also keeps the meeting focused on the task at hand, and avoids distractions such as the waiter interrupting.
>
> practical tip

What Is the Goal of the First Meeting?

The goal of your first prospect meeting is to learn more about the individual. Why is this person interested in the organization? For current donors, what motivated them to give? Is this individual interested in being more involved?

Another goal is to answer any questions the prospect might have about the organization and to give an overview of the good work you're doing. But as I stated above, be careful not to do all of the talking! This is a unique opportunity to learn about the prospect and get the person more involved. Ask open-ended questions, such as:

◆ What motivates you to give to this organization? For example, is there a history of cancer in your family? Why do you feel it is important to have a clean environment? What was it about your education here that impacted your life?

◆ Are you interested in being more involved with our organization, and in what capacity? Can I tell you more about some of the ways to become involved?

◆ Which of our programs is most interesting to you and why? What would you like to see us work on or do more of?

> **The Importance of Silence**
>
> The most important thing to do after making an ask, for a specific amount and a specific program or project, is to be quiet. The prospect must be the next person to speak. Why? Because if you start talking before the prospect has a chance to respond, there's a good chance you'll become nervous and backpedal. In other words, if you asked for $10,000, in the awkward silence that invariably follows an ask, you might blurt out "I know that's a lot. How about $5,000 instead?"
>
> practical tip

After the Meeting

You should never leave any meeting without a follow-up plan. Next steps can include setting up another meeting, a promise to send information, or agreeing to provide additional information by phone.

A true cultivation process (relationship building) might take many months, or even years, before getting to the solicitation stage, depending on the size of the gift you're seeking and the individual you're cultivating.

If you're just getting started (and working on *50 Asks in 50 Weeks*), you will want to ask for a gift within a year, every year, for your annual fund. (I'm assuming you're not in a capital campaign, and this is not a multiyear gift.)

Solicitation—the Ask Meeting

As we discussed in **Chapter Three,** when board members and executive directors say they don't want to fundraise, they're generally afraid of the "ask," or solicitation. They don't understand that fundraising is a process, and often think of it as making cold calls or begging for money.

Conquering Your Fear of Fundraising

I discuss fear of fundraising at length in *Major Gift Fundraising for Small Shops: How to Leverage Your Annual Fund in Only Five Hours per Week.* For the purpose of this chapter, here are a few suggestions to help your board and staff members overcome their fear or embarrassment:

◆ Remind them that fundraising isn't about the money—*it's about what the money will allow your organization to do for your community.* Money is just the tool you'll use to change lives, save lives, restore our environment, or whatever important work you do.

◆ When we ask donors to make gifts, we are giving them an opportunity to make a difference about a cause they care about. When we ask for major gifts, we're giving them the chance to leave a legacy they can be proud of. The one thing we're most certainly *not* doing is "begging" for money!

◆ It's not personal. This money is not for you. If you do get rejected—it's not you they are rejecting. They may have other causes they care about. Don't take it personally. Fundraising, like sales, is a numbers game. Keep asking until you get that desired "yes."

◆ Before going to ask someone for a gift, you should prepare by role playing with the other people who will be attending the meeting. Each person at the meeting should have a specific role. For example, the board member can thank the person for taking the time to meet and for the person's past support. Next, the executive director can remind the person of the impact that prior support has had on the program and discuss the progress that has been made this year. The executive director might also talk about the upcoming projects and what you hope to accomplish. Finally, the board member could wrap up the meeting by asking for a gift *in a specific amount.*

◆ Regardless of the agreed-upon roles, someone must be responsible for making the ask. However, as a staff member, you must be prepared to make the ask if the board member freezes during the meeting—which has been known to happen. Whatever you do, don't leave the meeting until the ask has been made. Have a transition phrase in mind to help you get to the ask if the end of the meeting is approaching and the ask hasn't been made.

practical tip

Who Is the Right Person to Make the Ask?

Ideally, the best person to make the ask is a board member who knows the prospect, is a peer of the prospect, and has been involved in the cultivation process. If a board member is unable or unwilling to do the asking, the member should at least be present during the meeting. After board members, the ask often falls to the executive director. Short of that, it falls to the development director.

The most important point, though, is to be sure that the person who plans to ask has a good relationship with the prospective donor and is ready and willing to make the ask.

How Much Should You Ask For?

Even though you've already determined your organization's major gift levels, when it comes to dealing with individual donors, the question of how much to ask for remains one of the most difficult questions to answer. Large development shops with dedicated research staff can often find out a great deal about an individual's assets and wealth. In your small shop, a good cultivation process, discussions about prospects with board members, and some basic online research will need to suffice.

Determining the ultimate ask amount depends on a variety of factors:

◆ What is the individual's giving history—both to your organization and to other nonprofits?

◆ Without too much research, what do you know about the person's lifestyle and assets? What type of job does the prospect have? What about the prospect's spouse or partner? Do they have children to support or college tuition to pay? How many vacation homes or what type of vacations do they take?

◆ During your cultivation discussions, what has the prospect expressed an interest in supporting? At what level?

◆ What do your board members have to say about this prospect's capacity to give?

Use the cultivation process to try to determine what level of gift might be achievable. You can do this by giving examples of things your organization needs. For example, ask if the person would be interested in supporting a staff salary in the $100,000 range, or a week of program services for $10,000.

When to Ask

You should ask for a gift as soon as you feel the person will say yes. Don't drag the process out unnecessarily! Most donors wonder why they keep having meetings without anyone asking them for support. Your organization needs the money now, so go ahead and ask.

Where to Ask

As I discussed briefly in the cultivation section, it's often difficult to hold a meeting in a restaurant—and restaurants are definitely *not* the place to ask for a gift! Just imagine being interrupted by a waiter or by a crash from the kitchen right as you're getting ready to ask. When speaking about something as sensitive as money, you should be in a quiet, confidential place where you can't be interrupted or overheard.

The best place to ask for a gift is wherever the prospect feels most comfortable. Often that's at home or at the office. If you've met there during the cultivation stage, asking in that setting should feel natural.

How to Ask

In my experience, asking for money is so difficult because we live in a society where talking about money is taboo. Here are some example asks to help get the words out:

◆ Board member to prospect: "As you know, I support the program with my time and my money to the greatest extent I am able. I hope you'll join me and consider making a gift in the range of $10,000 to support the afterschool program."

◆ Executive director to prospect: "As you know, it takes a lot of resources to help children stay safe, have fun, and continue to learn in an afterschool setting. I'm here to ask you to consider a gift in the range of $10,000 to support our afterschool program."

When you ask, ask for a certain amount. If you simply ask for support of the afterschool program, then a donor could give you $50 and have done what you asked. Ask for what you want, what you need, and what you believe the person will be able to give.

Soliciting major gifts from individuals is a lot of work, but the end result is worth the effort.

> **The Magic Phrase**
>
> When asking a donor for a gift, use the term "in the range of" and then provide *a single number.* In other words, don't actually give a range.
>
> I like to use the phrase "in the range of" when requesting a gift because it gives the person the opportunity to come back with a different amount rather than just a "yes" or "no." However, don't actually provide a range (such as $1,000 to $5,000), because most people automatically choose the lowest number.
>
> practical tip

Following Up

There are only three basic answers people can give when asked for a gift: Yes, no, or maybe. Before going to an ask meeting, you should be prepared to respond to any one of the three answers.

If you get a "yes," thank the donor and ask how he or she would like to make the gift. Should you provide an envelope for a check, or would a credit card be more convenient? Might it be a stock gift? Refer to your stewardship plan to set the appropriate thank-you process in place.

If you get a "maybe," be prepared with follow-up questions. What additional information do you need to provide? Does the donor need to check with a spouse or a financial advisor? Ask when you should follow up to find out the decision. Be specific. Say, "Could we schedule a time for me to call, or meet again next Thursday afternoon, to continue the conversation?"

Preparing to Hear "No"

There are many reasons that people say no when they're asked for a gift, in addition to the top two reasons we talked about in **Chapter Four.**

Some of the reasons that people say "no" include:

◆ I was asked by the wrong person. In other words, I like Joe, but he's not who I look up to or trust. This can be difficult to determine because your donor is unlikely to come out and say this.

◆ I was asked for the wrong project. In other words, I like the preschool center, but I'm really more interested in the afterschool program.

◆ I was asked at the wrong time. In other words, the stock market crashed, or I lost my job, or I have to pay for my child's wedding this year.

◆ I was asked for the wrong amount. In other words, I can't give that much, and I'm feeling uncomfortable giving less, or I could give more and want to do more than what you've asked.

> **Counting Your Asks**
>
> Start with a list of twenty major gift prospects.
>
> Include the top ten (from your list of twenty) whom you will ask for a gift within the next year in your overall 50 Asks plan. Be sure to create a cultivation plan for each person.

Most of these issues can be avoided by listening well during the cultivation process.

That said, be prepared for these reactions. For example, if the person says "I need to think about it," or "Not now," ask open-ended questions that might uncover the underlying reasons so you'll know how to proceed.

Remember: No doesn't mean never; it simply means not today. Your job is to keep the conversation going over time and eventually turn the "no" into a "yes."

Planned Giving

A planned gift is a donation to a charity that has tax implications or other benefits to the donor or donor's family beyond a basic charitable deduction. These gifts require planning on the part of the donor and often involve their accountants or attorneys. Examples of planned gifts include testamentary gifts (gifts at death that can be made by will or trust), annuities, life insurance, charitable trusts, or gifts of real estate.

If you're starting a planned giving program from scratch, the first step is to determine what type of gifts your organization can easily and practically accept. For example, a gift of fine art or property could cost more to maintain and sell than you'd actually receive from the sale, so your policy may state that your organization can't accept such gifts.

Once you've determined the types of gifts you can accept, publicize them! Create a section in your newsletter and on your website letting people know that you now accept certain types of planned gifts. If nothing else, you can certainly accept testamentary gifts and current gifts of stock!

Connect with an estate planning attorney through your board to provide language about testamentary gifts for your website newsletter. Ask current and former board members to be among the first to include your organization in their wills and trusts. This is something you can also discuss with your top major gift prospects and most loyal donors.

When discussing estate gifts with prospects, be sure to explain that you know that family comes first. However, don't hesitate to talk percentages. Explain that while the person might want to leave 80 or 90 percent of the estate to family, a gift of 5 or 10 percent would still make a positive impact on your cause. By giving a tangible example, prospects will understand that the bulk of their estate can still go to family *and* they will still be able to make a difference in the wider community.

Cultivation Plan

Name (Prospective Donor): _____

Main Contact(s) (on staff and board): _____

Ask Amount (Amount we hope to ask for): $_____

Ask Date (When we hope to ask by): _____

Month	Activity	Responsible Party	Status
January			
February			
March			
April			
May			
June			
July			
August			
September			
October			
November			
December			

Some Basic Steps for a Planned Giving Program

❑ Invite an estate planning attorney familiar with charitable planned gifts to help you create a gift acceptance committee (GAC) consisting of the attorney and other carefully-picked allied professionals, such as an accountant, banker, real estate agent, and so on. The GAC can advise the organization on setting policy, as well as review any particular gift transaction.

❑ Create a gift acceptance policy manual. It should carefully spell out what types of gifts your organization will consider accepting, and which it won't. It should also cover the procedures for considering and accepting any particular proposed planned gift. Creating the manual is a great first assignment for your GAC!

❑ Publicize the kinds of gifts your organization would like to receive.

❑ Invite past and present board members to include your organization in their wills and living trusts to kick off your planned giving program.

❑ Feature those who have in your newsletter and on your website as an example to others.

Check out "Leave a Legacy" at *leavealegacy.org* to learn more about the basics of leaving an estate gift to charity.

To Recap

◆ Major gift solicitation is a critical component of a solid development plan.

◆ Determine what a major gift is for your organization by using your database or thinking about gifts that have been cause for celebration.

◆ Your database and your board members are your sources for determining major gift prospects.

◆ Create cultivation plans for each individual prospect.

◆ Prepare for your ask meetings by using role playing and reminding participants that fundraising isn't about the money.

◆ Start a planned giving program by requesting testamentary gifts from board members and other supporters through personal requests and advertising the opportunity in your newsletter and on your website.

Chapter Eight

Grant Research, Writing, and Relationships

IN THIS CHAPTER

- ···→ Government grants—pros and cons

- ···→ How to research grants and pick the best opportunities

- ···→ Establishing and building relationships with foundations

- ···→ Writing grant proposals, attachments, and budgets

Grant seeking is probably the most popular form of fundraising for small nonprofits because the process is so predictable; the funder tells you exactly what to do and when to do it. However, I've found that small organizations rely too heavily on grant writing.

In reality, only a small percentage of the overall philanthropic dollars available come from grants. Also, small organizations frequently write and send in grants, but don't work on building relationships with the people at the foundations. (For our purposes in this chapter, I'm going to use the term "foundation" to refer to a wide variety of grant-making entities, including family, corporate, community, and other foundations.)

If your organization already gets more than 50 percent of its budget from grants, feel free to skim through this section to make sure that your grant writing is as efficient and effective as it could be. If you want to build better relationships with your funders, this will also be a good chapter for you to read.

Government Grants—Pros and Cons

On one hand, government grants—whether federal, state, or local—can generate enormous sums of money. On the other, government grants are often highly competitive, challenging to complete, and require huge amounts of reporting. The work involved is frequently not worth it for smaller organizations.

Not only that, but government funding has been shrinking on all levels since 2008, and that trend is likely to continue. Also, the priorities of all levels of our government tend to change with each election, making this kind of funding highly unreliable.

Given these variables, this chapter won't be discussing government funding—even though this type of funding can be very lucrative for nonprofits with the staff to compete for and manage it.

Researching Grants to Find the Right Fit

How do you identify the foundations you will apply to each year? Do you actively research the possibilities, or do you wait until foundations are brought to your attention? Given what you've seen in the rest of this book, I think you can guess which approach I recommend.

The obvious place to start is to reapply to those foundations from which you've received funding in the past. After you've done that, though, the challenge of identifying new foundations begins.

There are several good places to research grant opportunities. My favorite is the Foundation Center: *foundationcenter.org.*

To get started with the Foundation Center, you can access its basic free database online. To do more in-depth research for free, though, you'll need to visit one of its many partner institutions, which are frequently located in public or university libraries. (Check the Foundation Center's website for a current listing of locations, and call before going to make sure someone is available to show you how to use the database.) You can also pay to have access to its full database from your desktop.

Don't let yourself become overwhelmed by grant research. There's no need for you to spend all year researching and constantly adding foundations to your list. After all, grant writing and grant administration are time-intensive processes. If you try to raise your entire yearly budget this way you won't have time for anything else, let alone getting yourself up to fifty asks! Instead, set aside one or two days to do all of your grant research for that year.

In just one day spent researching, you should find several foundations you've never heard of which could be great prospects for your organization.

To find the foundations that are the *best* matches, be sure to read and follow their guidelines and requirements exactly. For instance, if a foundation only funds organizations in New York and your organization is in Texas, don't waste your time. I know this seems obvious, but you wouldn't believe the number of times applicants ignore these basic pieces of information.

Likewise, if you're looking for funding for a children's program, it's possible at first glance to think you've found a match. But look more closely. You may find out that the foundation supports programs for teens while your nonprofit serves preschoolers.

After identifying as many prospective foundations as you can, continue your research by looking up each individual foundation's website to get as much additional information as possible. Look for grant guidelines, deadlines, contact information, and program priorities.

Think of it this way. Reviewing a prospective foundation's website is the first step in starting your relationship with that organization. Just as you want to supplement your online research about individual donors by asking the donors about themselves, you also want to see what the foundations you're looking at have to say about their own missions, histories, and priorities.

Do not rely on third party sources or donor databases (including the Foundation Center) for information. Go directly to each individual foundation's website for specific guidelines, application information, and deadlines.

But Is It a Perfect Match?

After your initial research is complete, it's time to rank the foundations you've identified to decide which ones you'll apply to this year as part of your 50 Asks plan:

◆ *Perfect match.* "A's" are foundations whose missions match yours. "A" foundations also give in your geographic area and provide the type of funding you're looking for.

◆ *Good match.* "B" foundations share some overlap in mission and geography with your nonprofit, but they also fund a wide variety of other programs and/or locations. Or, after reviewing their website or talking to someone who knows the foundation, you may have a hunch that it isn't the best fit.

◆ *Remote match.* "C's" are the foundations that at first glance seemed to be a match, but with additional research turn out not to be a match after all. For example, as mentioned above, you might need funds for a preschool program but find out the foundation makes grants to support teens.

After throwing the C's away, file the B's for a rainy day. If you have enough in the "A" category to last you the year, then you're finished. If you can handle more foundations than you have in your "A" pile, you have more research to do.

On the other hand, if you have more funders in the "A" pile than you can handle in one year, sort them by how much they give. There's no reason to apply to a lot of smaller foundations that each gives $1,000 if you've identified sufficient funders that give $10,000 or more.

When you're making your final selections, you'll need to determine how many re-applications plus new applications you can accomplish each year. (And remember to ask for help from other staff members and volunteers!) As a part of your 50 Asks program, make a goal to write at least one grant application per month.

How to Find a Match

While The Foundation Center provides guides to using its database, here are some threshold questions to get you started:

❑ Does the foundation provide support in your geographic area? Some foundations make grants to organizations regardless of where they're located, but most foundations restrict their giving to one or two states, counties, or even countries.

❑ Does it fund your type of organization or program? Ask yourself: "Is my organization a good match for this foundation's mission?"

❑ Does it provide the type of funding you are looking for, for example, unrestricted, program, salary, capital, or endowment?

If you can answer "yes" to these questions, you have a potential match.

practical tip

Finally, before making your final selections, talk with your staff and board to see if any of them know any staff and/or board members at the foundations on your "A" list. If so, ask that staff person or board member to help jump-start your organization's relationship with these particular foundations.

Grant Applications

	Foundation Name	Application Deadline	Amount	Contact Requested	Notes/Info
1					
2					
3					
4					
5					
6					
7					
8					
9					
10					
11					
12					
13					
14					
15					

Creating Your Grant Writing Schedule

After your research is complete, sort your list by due date. If most of the foundations you will apply to have specific due dates, add those dates to your calendar. However, many foundations accept applications year-round or have multiple deadlines.

That said, even most foundations that accept applications year-round or at multiple points throughout the year have "better" times for receiving applications. For example, some foundations give away much more funding during their first grant cycle of the year than during their last yearly cycle, when they may be running low on funds. So while you're filling in your grant writing "asks" on your 50 Asks calendar, be sure to pick the best times to apply to these organizations.

Also, most foundations that accept applications year-round probably have internal cut-off deadlines before board meetings that occur annually, semiannually, or quarterly. If you unknowingly miss one of these deadlines it could take six months or more for the foundation to review your application. If you learn the foundation's internal deadline schedule and get your application in ahead of time, you could get your answer in as little as six weeks! (We'll discuss how to get this information in the next section.)

Building Relationships with Foundation Funders

Many years ago, a foundation program officer told me that most applicants never contacted him or his foundation except by submitting a grant application. And, if the nonprofit received funding, it often submitted the required reports, but nothing more.

The speaker went on to say that he *liked* speaking to potential and current grantees and was puzzled that more development officers and executive directors weren't contacting him with questions.

If you've never thought to pick up the phone and introduce yourself to your funders, you should! A foundation program officer's job is to get to know nonprofits and support them. If you don't call, how can you build a relationship?

Before that long-ago seminar, I was too intimidated to contact foundations. I was convinced that no one would take my call! But the speaker was so insistent about his desire to interact with nonprofits that I went back to my office the next day and picked up the phone.

The results were remarkable! After calling three foundations that month, I got new first-time funding from each one. For me, this was a huge improvement—and it happened because I talked with the program officers, asked them questions, and refined my applications according to their answers.

If you think your organization is a good match for a specific foundation, call and speak with a program officer to see if you are right. You can also ask about application deadlines, including the internal deadlines I mentioned above.

Before calling, make a list of your questions. For example:

◆ *I understand that you fund children's programs, and our organization runs afterschool programs. We're thinking of applying for tutors for three of our largest programs. Does that sound like something that would interest your foundation?*

◆ *We have several programs that might be a good match for your foundation. Can you tell me which you think sounds like the best match?* (Then proceed to have quick descriptions of each program.)

◆ *Your website says you accept applications year-round, but is there a better time of year to apply? When does your board meet to review applications? Do you have a larger pot of money to give at the beginning of the year?*

◆ *Are you planning to make grants to new organizations this year?*

◆ *Do you have advice for a new applicant?*

◆ *When are decisions made?*

◆ *When could we expect to hear about a decision?*

After an initial conversation, the next time to call is one week after you mail your application. Confirm that the foundation received it, and ask if there are any questions. Most program officers won't have questions by that time (or even know if your application arrived yet) but the call is the next step in building your relationship.

These before-and-after phone calls have proven to be highly productive for me. Even though most program officers simply say they haven't gotten to the applications yet, I'm confident that the calls raise officers' awareness, who then take the time to thoroughly review my application. By calling, I've reminded them that I am diligent, and my application stands out when they get to it. My first few calls are usually so positive that I would never consider *not* calling a foundation now.

I'm frequently asked about foundations that don't advertise their phone numbers, or that proactively say they don't take calls. This generally happens with small foundations (a family foundation without staff, for example) that don't have the capacity to answer calls.

In these circumstances I try to find a connection to the foundation, such as through one of my board members who knows one of the foundation's board members, to make an introduction. Social networking is also great for these types of circumstances; you might be connected to someone at the foundation on LinkedIn or Facebook or be able to get an introduction through someone you know.

When foundations don't have staff members publish their phone numbers, I have gone as far as looking up the work phone numbers or emails of their board members. Generally, the board members have taken my call. And when they don't, so what? I'm no worse off than I was before I picked up the phone.

As with all fundraising, your chances of receiving a grant will significantly increase if you have a relationship with the funder. Even if a particular foundation decides not to fund your organization, building a relationship with them enables you to ask if they could introduce you to other foundations that might be a better match. Also, not getting funding the first time doesn't mean you shouldn't apply again.

Writing Proposals

Applying for grants can be challenging, but if you've written out in advance all the basic pieces of information you'll need, each application is generally a relatively simple cut-and-paste job. Each application needs to be tailored to the specifications of the funder, of course, but in most cases, you probably have a majority of the information and attachments on hand. I've listed the most common required information later in this chapter.

I always use a hard copy of the guidelines, printed out from the website. I highlight, circle, or underline the important items, such as deadlines, specific page number requirements, spacing and binding requirements, font type and size, and attachments. After completing the grant, I refer back to my highlights to make sure I have done everything required and have included all the necessary attachments, before mailing or emailing it in. Most importantly, I stick to deadlines.

An important component of grant seeking is remembering to answer the questions *as they are asked*. If you cut and paste a paragraph from a different grant application, make sure it actually answers the question being asked in *this* application. Use examples, stories, and statistics whenever possible.

Don't fabricate or exaggerate numbers of clients served or budget numbers. Foundations generally know what's possible with a given amount of funding. Even if you do get the grant, it's unlikely that you'll have the predicted results at the end of the year, and you'll probably lose the grant the next year.

> **Yes, Grant Applications Count!**
>
> Add the number of grants you plan to apply for to your total asks for the year.
>
>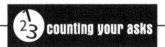

Finally, have someone outside of your organization review your grant applications to make sure they make sense to someone who isn't familiar with your program and that they answer the questions asked.

Attachments

There is some basic information that almost all foundations require. I recommend having a grant file on your computer with an "attachments" folder, where you keep all of your attachments readily accessible and available for attaching or printing for an application. This list includes, but is not limited to:

◆ Organization mission statement

◆ Organization history

◆ Project summary

◆ Audited financial statements

◆ 501(c)(3) IRS Determination Letter

◆ Most recent annual report

◆ Project budget

◆ Organization budget

◆ List of board members with affiliations

Funding Request and Budgeting

How much should you ask for from foundation funders?

To determine how much to ask for, look at the foundation's grants from the past two years. These figures are often available on a foundation's website or in its annual report. If the foundation gives to many programmatic areas, focus on the area in which you'll be applying.

> **Let Them See You in Action**
>
> To develop a relationship with a foundation, you could invite the program officer for a tour and offer to send materials about your organization before submitting your application. Don't worry if the officer says "no" the first time you ask—now the officer knows that you're open to the idea.
>
>

Getting Started with Grants

❑ Research foundations.

❑ Rank your findings "A," "B," and "C."

❑ Decide which of your "A" foundations you'll apply to based on how much they give.

❑ Fill in your grant calendar.

❑ Call foundations to build relationships and ask questions.

❑ Apply for grants.

In your application, ask for an amount in the middle of the foundation's giving range, especially if your organization would be a first-time grantee. You rarely want to ask for the most—or, for that matter, the least—the foundation typically gives.

The amount you ask for also depends on how much your program costs. Very few funders want to be a project's sole supporter, so if your project budget is $30,000, target three foundations for $10,000 each.

Additionally, each foundation has its own rules about what it will and won't fund. Some allow a percentage of operating funds. If so, ask for that percentage. Many foundations will make grants that include salary line items.

Knowing the answers to these questions in advance won't just help with your application—it will also help your budgeting process. Coordinate with the person in your office who handles budgets to come up with a project budget that works within the framework of your overall organizational budget.

Follow Up

Congratulations—you've been awarded the grant! Send a thank-you letter now! You might also want to call or email the program officer you have built a relationship with, especially if you're not the person signing the thank-you letter.

For Lack of a Paper Clip, the Grant Was Lost

When preparing to write a grant application, first *review and follow the application guidelines.* Many otherwise good applications have been tossed in the trash because of technical errors—not enough copies, a staple instead of a paper clip, single spacing instead of double… even some sent by email when a hard copy is required.

If these criteria sound overly picky to you, remember—the foundations you're applying to receive hundreds, or even perhaps thousands, of applications every year. Just as you want to meet with major donor prospects in locations that are most comfortable to them, you also want to make it as easy as possible for foundation funders to review your application.

Most, if not all, foundations post their guidelines on their websites. Don't rely on third parties like the Foundation Center for this information. Foundations often have much more extensive information on their own website or in their materials than is listed elsewhere. If a foundation doesn't have a website, call to ask for grant guidelines.

Just as you have with your individual major donors, create a calendar of cultivation and stewardship "events" for the year to further build your relationships with your foundation funders. For the most part, this means including your foundation funders in your existing stewardship calendar, but there are a few extra steps you'll want to take with the foundations themselves. For example:

◆ Send newsletters as well as your annual report and other publications.

◆ Send articles whenever your organization appears in the news.

◆ Send e-blasts and regular updates.

◆ Invite program officers to visit your program two to three times per year, such as for a tour, fundraising events, and client events.

◆ Send all requested reports on time.

And, most importantly,

◆ Send a letter, email, or call with an update if there is a change to the program or project a particular foundation is funding, especially if there is a problem or delay with the project.

If you didn't receive a grant from any foundations you believe are truly a good match for your organization, include these funders in your cultivation activities anyway and apply again next year. Call the program officers to thank the foundations for considering your application, and ask for any feedback they might have to help you improve.

Finding a Foundation Connection

Use social media to increase your chances of creating relationships at the foundations you're targeting. For example, use LinkedIn or Facebook to discover if anyone you know is acquainted with the person you're interested in contacting at a specific foundation.

practical tip

How Much Should You Ask For?

If last year the foundation gave one hundred grants of $10,000, one hundred grants of $25,000, and three grants of $100,000, ask for $25,000.

In this example, $100,000 seems to be the exception to the rule. On the other hand, the foundation is obviously extremely comfortable giving $25,000.

Example

To Recap

◆ Each year, take a day to actively research new grant opportunities.

◆ Increase your chances of receiving grants by building relationships with foundation funders.

◆ If you have more grant opportunities than you have time to apply for, prioritize those you have relationships with and those that give the most money per grant.

◆ Submit grant proposals exactly as requested by the funder, and be sure to answer questions as asked.

◆ Keep your documents with the most-requested information readily available to make the grant application process as efficient as possible.

◆ Cultivate and steward your foundation funders as you do your individual donors.

Chapter Nine

Events Aren't About Ticket Sales, They're About Sponsorships

IN THIS CHAPTER

-----→ Making your events are as efficient and effective as possible

-----→ Sponsorships, not tickets, are the key to generating revenue

-----→ Building a fundraising committee to help

-----→ Following up with prospects

Some of you will see this as the fun chapter. Others will dread reading it. Why? Because while events can be fun to do, they're also a lot of work. And without a proper focus, it's all too common for nonprofits to host events that lose money or barely break even.

I'm going to remind you of one of the most important points of this book: Fundraising is a team sport. This includes events. In other words, you don't have to (and shouldn't!) try to organize all of your organization's fundraising events any more than you should work on bulk mail, grants, or major gifts alone.

Event Pros and Cons

There are many pros and cons to having special events. As I mentioned above, events are labor intensive, requiring many hours of work by both staff and volunteers. Event fundraising is also the most expensive way to raise money. So why do we have them?

◆ Events are unique occasions to showcase your organization to your current supporters and get your message out to the wider community.

◆ Events are opportunities to raise a lot of money from companies and individuals who might not otherwise give.

◆ Events can be great for cultivating prospects.

◆ Events build your database.

◆ The funds you raise from events are unrestricted, so they can be used for operating expenses.

For these reasons, and despite the work involved, I'm convinced that all nonprofits should have at least one fundraising event every year. I also strongly caution organizations that have many small events throughout the year that the effort involved renders them inefficient. Consider these drawbacks:

◆ Events are the most expensive type of fundraising—often raising $1 for every $.50 spent.

◆ Events are extremely labor intensive.

◆ If not planned carefully, an event can lose money or make a bad impression on the very people you are trying to impress.

Be Creative

In the past, you couldn't go wrong with a gala or golf outing, but things have changed. Today, it's important to have a unique event, where people have the opportunity to experience your organization. How can you create an experience, so people want to come back to your event year after year—and bring their friends? How can your attendees feel good and have fun?

How can you help bring your organization to life for your donors? Here are some examples:

◆ If your organization provides clean water, can you have guests simulate getting water from a well or other water source? Is the water safe to drink? How would they know? Have them carry containers of water (on their heads). Raffle off opportunities for clean water, rather than gift certificates, jewelry, or art.

> ### Keep the Best, Cut the Rest
>
> Due to the effort and expense required for most special events, I encourage small nonprofits to host only one, or at most two, events per year. If your nonprofit can't afford to dedicate at least one full-time staff person to events, closely analyze each event to discover which ones actually make money. Cancel any that aren't cost-effective and put all your time and resources into the top one or two most successful events.
>
>  practical tip

◆ If your organization is a school, can you have guests play educational computer games or experience the latest teaching techniques, science labs, or art studios? What about an outdoor classroom? How can you bring their experience to life? Raffle off scholarships, so each guest can send one child to your school for free for a week, a month, or a year.

◆ If your organization is a healthcare organization, how can you bring the patient experience to life while being sensitive to guests who actually have those diseases? Can you have a game show and ask guests questions? Or have scenarios where they make tough decisions?

The bottom line is that events should be *fun*! People should have a great feeling about your organization at the end of the event and want to come back year after year. Guests should also leave knowing more about your organization than when they arrived without having been bored with long speeches. If you can do that, you have done your job well.

Start with a Budget

The first step in determining whether to have an event is to create a revenue and expense budget. How much will this type of event cost and how much do you think you can (realistically) raise?

How much will the event cost? Some sample budget items are:

- ◆ Venue

- ◆ Food

- ◆ Entertainment

- ◆ Decorations

- ◆ Invitations and postage

- ◆ Ad book/program

- ◆ Photographer/videographer

- ◆ Audiovisual equipment

> **Eating for a Good Cause**
>
> Every year, a group of our friends joins my husband and me in attending a fundraiser for a soup kitchen, a project of a culinary school. The school has recruited about thirty restaurants to donate small plates, so it doesn't pay for the food. Also, the school has its graduates and attendees showcase their skills and food at various booths. It's a truly amazing event—one that we are eager to attend every year.

stories from the real world

It's important to keep expenses as low as possible. Donors don't want charities to spend all their money on throwing parties.

It's equally important to know how much you can raise. Try creating a minimum/maximum revenue budget. For example, if you may know you can get at least fifty people to attend, and you hope to have one hundred, those numbers would dictate your minimum and maximum revenue. Likewise, you should identify at least three potential sponsors for each sponsorship you actually expect to get. For example, you could plan for one sponsorship at the $10,000 level if the committee knows three individuals or companies who might realistically give at that level.

Sell Sponsorships, Not Tickets

Selling individual event tickets is labor intensive. The same principle holds true, in fact, for any item that must be sold one at a time (candy sales, bake sales, car washes, etc.).

These types of activities are bad fundraising events for any small organization. Not only are they labor intensive, but they also don't raise a lot of money.

Sponsorships can raise significant amounts of money with much less work. The organizations I work with always have a ticket price for the individuals who want to buy them—but our main focus is on selling entire tables and sponsorship packages.

We keep the focus on sponsorships because events are another example of the Pareto principle: 20 percent of your donors will give 80 percent of the money you raise while 80 percent of them will contribute 20 percent to your event's bottom line. To "ask smart," then, we need to focus on that top 20 percent by selling sponsorships.

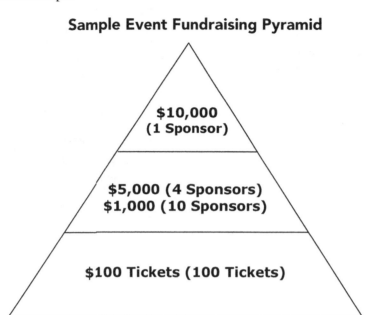

Sample Event Fundraising Pyramid

$10,000
(1 Sponsor)

$5,000 (4 Sponsors)
$1,000 (10 Sponsors)

$100 Tickets (100 Tickets)

Selecting an Event Committee

The purpose of an event committee is to help you raise money.

I know this sounds obvious, but it's a novel concept to most organizations. Most event committees *spend* money instead of raising it. Rather than focusing on bringing funds in, they concentrate on planning the event and spend money on invitations, centerpieces, giveaways, music, food, photographers…the list goes on and on. If your nonprofit has an event committee that spends rather than raises money, it's time to "fire" the volunteers and start fresh.

How do you start the transition to an event committee that's dedicated to fundraising? By having the event chair, executive director, or development director make a clear statement of the fundraising goal for this year's event and request a commitment from each committee member to achieve that goal by personally raising money. You can then ask past committee members to commit to the new expectations or to step down. Honestly and carefully explain that this year's event needs to be different and that you need a different kind of help to succeed.

Some of your existing committee members will stick around and rise to the challenge. Others will

Keeping Volunteers Happy

As your *non*fundraising committee members start slipping away, you will probably want to offer at least some of them the opportunity to serve your nonprofit in a different capacity. Obviously, you'll want to make this determination on a case-by-case basis. The point is, do everything you can to make this a "win-win" situation for these volunteers and for your nonprofit.

practical tip

naturally, and quietly, slip away. You may want to keep volunteers who can generate in-kind donations and get you access to other resources, such as free printing. Also, I understand that you might have one or two individuals whom you will want to keep around because they love to plan events, or a volunteer you want to keep happy for political reasons. However, from now on, call the event committee the "Event *Fundraising* Committee."

Finally, take some of the control back into your organization's hands. Decisions like menu, vendors, and location should be left with a staff member or a highly trustworthy volunteer. All of these changes will ensure you won't lose money before the event even begins.

Now that you know the real purpose of your event committee, what, specifically, should its members do? Ideally, you should have people with recognizable names who probably will not do much work but who will raise money, plus some "worker bees" who aren't names in your community but who will also be able to bring in one or two sponsorships.

Let committee members know up front that you expect them to buy or sell at least one table or sponsorship. If your committee has ten members, by the time you're done recruiting them, you will have already sold ten tables!

Don't forget to lay out additional expectations, such as:

- ◆ Attending two meetings
- ◆ Helping to develop a concept for an original, unique, and fun event
- ◆ Helping to select and recruit speakers and honorees
- ◆ Helping to set sponsorship levels and ticket prices

At this point you may be thinking, "Amy is out of her mind! We'll *never* be able to recruit people to serve on a committee like that!" The good news is that these types of roles give committee members a sense of ownership in the event.

Planning and Timelines

Almost a year in advance, select the type of event you will have, a date, and a location with the help of your committee.

Keep in mind that the most popular seasons for events are spring and fall. When choosing your date, avoid conflicts by first finding out what other popular events are happening in the same time frame. Once you select a date and time, clear both with your committee and board members. Next on the to-do list is selecting honorees and speakers (if you have them) and getting the date on their calendars as well.

The planning keeps going throughout the year. See the sidebar on the next page for a detailed timeline of what to do when.

Selecting Honorees

If you choose to hold an awards event, selecting the right honorees is a critical step to your fundraising success. Selecting the right people will buy and sell sponsorships for you as well as draw additional guests.

Staff and volunteers should think of companies, individuals, foundations, and groups that support your organization. Some of your committee members may have access to people you wouldn't ordinarily

Basic Event Timeline

One Year Before Event

- ❑ Recruit committee
- ❑ Determine type of event
- ❑ Select date and book venue
- ❑ Select honorees (if appropriate) and speakers
- ❑ Develop budget

Six to Eight Months Out

- ❑ Determine sponsorship levels and benefits
- ❑ Set ticket prices
- ❑ Solicit key sponsors

Four to Six Months Out

- ❑ Solicit all sponsors
- ❑ Reconfirm with speakers and honorees
- ❑ Design invitation and ad book
- ❑ Plan raffle, silent auction, etc.

Two to Four Months Out

- ❑ Mail invitations
- ❑ Continue to solicit and follow up with sponsors
- ❑ Order any awards and plaques
- ❑ Get bios and photos from honorees
- ❑ Collect ads and logos for ad book
- ❑ Order and mail invitations

One Month Out

- ❑ Send press release
- ❑ Finalize ad book
- ❑ Confirm with vendors (venue, music, etc.)

Week of Event

- ❑ Finalize numbers with venue
- ❑ Print name tags
- ❑ Make table assignments
- ❑ Assign staff and board roles
- ❑ Match board greeters with donors/prospects
- ❑ Call local news outlets to get your event on their schedule

Week After

- ❑ Send thank-you letters to all donors, honorees, and committee members
- ❑ Make thank-you calls to all key volunteers and donors
- ❑ Schedule follow-up with prospects

reach, such as a local celebrity, politician, or head of a local company. Consider which honorees have the capacity and inclination to bring in funds, and make the decision of whom to honor as a committee, with staff recommendations guiding the process.

Next, decide who would be the best person to approach potential honorees. Let the potential honorees know what you expect of them up front, such as buying and selling sponsorships, providing a list of contacts to send invitations to, or making a speech at the event. Finally, make sure honorees have reserved the event date on their calendars.

Soliciting Sponsors

Soliciting sponsors is the most critical component of your event's success. One or two sponsors can generate the same amount of revenue as one hundred tickets.

Before you solicit sponsors, though, it's important to set sponsorship levels—and it's crucial to set them correctly. That's why your committee members need to play a role: they're charged with buying and selling sponsorships, so they need to set levels which will allow them to do just that.

Sponsorship levels can range from $500 to $50,000 or more, depending on the reach and capacity of your committee. Staff should make suggestions and guide the discussions, but the committee needs to be comfortable with at least the bottom level sponsorship amount. Once a comfort zone is established, decide on three sponsorship levels, with the top level being a real stretch.

Knowing When the Levels Are Right

If you get one or two sponsors at your top level, the amount they give should be large enough that you go screaming down the halls of your office with excitement. If you don't get any at that level, though, it's not a big deal. You should still be able to get one to three sponsors in the middle level and at least five to ten at the bottom level. If you do this, you'll know that you've set your levels well.

 practical tip

If It's Easy, You Can Do Better

Years ago, an organization hired me to help it with its annual fundraising event. I started by analyzing its sponsors and sponsorship levels from prior events. What I found was that the event had been raising approximately $50,000 annually, including $40,000 in sponsorship, plus ticket sales, silent auction, and journal ads. The top sponsorship opportunity was $5,000, and there were about eight sponsors at that top level. This immediately raised a red flag for me. If the nonprofit was able to get eight sponsors at its top level, that level was clearly too low.

Although the staff and board resisted raising their sponsorship levels, I convinced them to try a top level of $15,000, a middle level of $10,000, and a bottom level of $5,000. Even if they received no additional sponsorships, most of the old sponsors would still return at the $5,000 level.

As it turned out, the organization sold three sponsors at the new top level ($15,000) for a total of $45,000, and two sponsors at the $10,000 level for an additional $20,000. From these first five donors (sponsors) alone, the nonprofit raised $65,000—more than it had ever raised at the event before! This was before a single ticket, journal ad, or silent-auction item was sold. The event went on to raise well over $100,000—more than twice the usual amount.

 stories from the real world

Companies and individuals expect to receive recognition and benefits in return for their sponsorship. Seek committee members' help in determining what type of recognition they and their companies would want. Here are some standard examples:

Benefactor (Gold)

- One front row, premier table of ten
- Full page (or front or back inside cover) in ad journal/program
- Table sign with your name
- Recognition from the podium at the event
- Logo on organization's website for one year with link to company's website
- Premier signage at the event
- Company logo on invitation

Supporter (Silver)

- One table of ten
- Half-page in the ad journal/program
- Table sign with your name
- Recognition from the podium at the event
- Listing on organization's website for one year with link to company's website
- Listing on invitation

Friend Sponsor (Bronze)

- Two tickets
- Listing in the ad journal/program
- Table sign with your name

Don't give away so much that you lose money! I shouldn't have to say this, but a low-level sponsor should not get ten tickets to your event...two or four at the most.

Instead, think of benefits for sponsorship that are low cost or no cost. How much does it cost you to include a company's logo on your website or mention them from the podium at your event? Not much! It's an easy, yet valuable, benefit to give away.

To generate the most sponsorship dollars for your event, you'll need to begin soliciting sponsorships months before the invitations go out. Sponsorship solicitations aren't something you simply list on the event invitation. Instead, create separate sponsorship materials and send them specifically to potential sponsors, along with phone calls and follow-up calls or emails from a contact within your organization—often a committee member.

XYZ Organization
Sponsorship Form

Event Date and Time Location	Honorees and Speakers Listed Here Event Sponsors Listed Here

Name _____   Company Name _____

Address _____

Phone _____   Email _____

Sponsorship Opportunities

☐   Gold Sponsor $10,000
    ✓   Table of 10 (10 Tickets)
    ✓   Premium Full Page Ad in Program (back or inside covers)
    ✓   Name and Logo on Signage at Event
    ✓   Logo and Link on Website for One Year
    ✓   Name on Invitation (if committed by print deadline)

☐   Silver Sponsor $5,000
    ✓   Table of 10 (10 Tickets)
    ✓   Full Page Ad in Program
    ✓   Name and Logo on Signage at Event
    ✓   Name on Invitation (if committed by print deadline)

☐   Bronze Sponsor $2,500
    ✓   Two Tickets
    ✓   Half Page Ad in Program

Journal Ads

☐ Full Page $X,XXX   ☐ Half Page Ad $XXX   ☐ Quarter Page $XXX

Please Make Checks Payable To: XYZ Organization

Name (on Credit Card) _____   Credit Card Number _____

Expiration Date _____   Security Code _____

Signature _____

Please Return Form To: XYZ Organization at Address of Organization

Questions? Please Call Susan at 123-456-7890

Event Asks (Sponsorship)

	Prospect Name (Company/Individual)	Committee Member Contact	Ask Amount	Response/ Amount
Example	Company XYZ	Jane Smith	$5,000	Yes/$2,500
1				
2				
3				
4				
5				
6				
7				
8				
9				
10				
11				
12				
13				
14				
15				

TOTAL REQUESTED: $ _____

TOTAL RECEIVED: $ _____

Day of the Event

The day you've been planning for almost a year has finally arrived. Assign board members to greet VIPs and guests as they arrive. Assign someone to personally thank each sponsor.

A colleague once told me that she color codes name tags so board members know who they're supposed to connect with and can find them easily. One board member is responsible for greeting people with blue name tags, another for green, another for red, etc. This doesn't mean that board members shouldn't greet everyone, but they need to specifically find and welcome those who are assigned to them.

Follow Up

If you were able to get important prospects to attend your event, following up with them could be the most important part of the entire event. Make sure you follow up within a week with these people, as they will still be glowing with good feelings about your organization. Call them quickly to schedule a tour of your facility or visit them at their home or office. Turn them into individual prospects if they're not already part of your formal major gift plan. Don't lose your momentum!

To Recap

◆ Events provide the opportunity to raise unrestricted dollars for your organization, showcase your organization, build your database, and raise donations from those who might not otherwise give.

◆ Evaluate your events to determine which ones are worth the time and expense you're putting into them, and cancel the ones that aren't.

◆ Develop a fundraising committee to sell sponsorships and tickets, not spend money or plan the event.

◆ Starting one year in advance, plan your events and create a revenue and expense budget.

◆ Follow up with VIP prospects who attend.

Don't Panic—Really

Something will most likely go wrong at any event you host. Stay calm. Getting hysterical or screaming at people does nothing to enhance the event—or the situation.

On the night before an event I was running several years ago, a thunderstorm knocked the power out to the entire area. The event venue didn't have power. The refrigerators were out, and the food was going bad. The venue rented generators the size of trucks, but didn't have them up and running until thirty minutes before the guests arrived. And guess what? The guests never knew there was a problem!

Another time I hired a consultant to help me run an event. This consultant ended up screaming at the venue staff—in front of my guests. You can be sure that I never hired that consultant again!

stories from the real world

Chapter Ten

For Executive Directors Only

IN THIS CHAPTER

···→ Your role as chief fundraiser

···→ Working with your board on fundraising

···→ How and when to hire your first development staff member

···→ First-year expectations

Why a chapter for executive directors alone? In my experience, most nonprofit executive directors don't have any formal fundraising training. In particular, executive directors in small shops seldom have the time or the budget to pursue fundraising training while on the job.

Also, as the person in charge of your organization, you have a unique role in securing your nonprofit's bottom line, including acting as the cheerleader for your board and volunteers and, eventually, bringing on your first development staff person. With that in mind, I've written this chapter to help everyone, from the nonprofit executive directors who are doing it all themselves to those of you who are fortunate enough to have a staff to work with.

Finally, I encourage board members and other staff to review this chapter as well to develop a deeper understanding of your executive director's role.

Your Role as Chief Fundraiser

If your career has taken the same path as many executive directors, you started out as a direct worker in your field—full of passion, creativity, and compassion. Perhaps you were a teacher, social worker, or program director. But over the years, you were promoted and became a supervisor, a position for which you may or may not have received any real training.

Finally, you ended up taking the helm, whether by starting an organization yourself or stepping up to run an existing small nonprofit.

My point is, if you're like many executive directors working for small nonprofits, you've risen to your current position without much, if any, management training—and almost certainly none in fundraising. You might well find yourself pining for your days in the trenches!

The job of this entire workbook, and particularly this chapter, is to make your job a little easier.

If you've read this workbook chapter by chapter, you already know that you're critical to your organization's fundraising success. If you're starting with this chapter, I'll repeat myself: fundraising should take half your time.

If you're fortunate enough to have fundraising staff, raising money is still one of your major responsibilities, whether you're doing it yourself, getting your board to do it, or supervising development staff. If you don't have any fundraising staff, it's likely you are responsible for your nonprofit's bottom line. But just because you're responsible doesn't mean that you are the only one who needs to be raising money. Fundraising is a team sport!

How to Get Your Board on Board

I've discussed your board's role as fundraisers in depth in **Chapter Three.** For our purposes in this chapter, the most important thing for you to remember about getting your board members on the fundraising bandwagon is that you need to recruit them properly and set up realistic and honest expectations. Don't recruit them onto the board and then ambush them with fundraising expectations! If you don't establish the terms of their service from the start, both you and your board members are bound to be disappointed.

If you're currently working with a nonfundraising board, your job is twofold: recruit new members and change the culture of the board as a whole. Using the strategies I've laid out in **Chapter Three,** you can expect it to take about three years before you've seen sufficient turnover to effect a substantial change in your board's culture.

Besides the more detailed strategies in **Chapter Three,** here's your opening move. Find one current board member with influence who supports the idea of getting the board involved with fundraising. Explain the direction you'd like to take your organization—and why you need the board's help to make it happen. Then ask the member to meet with a few other like-minded members before the board meeting where you plan to bring up the issue.

In that meeting, have your chosen board member lead a discussion about increased board participation. The idea will have preplanted supporters—and you'll slowly start changing the culture of your organization.

Orienting New Board Members

The easiest way to change your board's culture, however, is to orient new board members properly.

Manage Your Board

Although board members are technically your superiors, as the executive director it's actually your responsibility to manage them.

I know executive directors who are so afraid of their boards that they let their board president run all over them. But as executive director, it's your responsibility to guide and make recommendations to your board, while at the same time taking advantage of their expertise, experience, and connections.

While the board/executive director relationship is a balancing act, it's important for the executive director, as the person who is most intimately involved with the day-to-day work, to lead both the board and the organization.

!
important

To help your new board members get off on the right foot, create an orientation packet that outlines your expectations for them. You might include:

◆ Information about your organization, including recent annual reports, newsletters, brochures, or videos

◆ Organization history and mission

◆ Budget

◆ Bylaws

◆ Strategic plan

◆ Calendar of events and meetings

◆ Board member job description

◆ Board member expectation form

◆ Board member conflict-of-interest form

◆ Committee descriptions and expectations

Board Member Expectation Form

The most important piece in that orientation packet is the board member expectation form. It's a comprehensive list of expectations that ensures that board members understand what's expected of them. This concept can be introduced at a board meeting or retreat and then provided to all incoming board members. The form should be updated and filled out by each board member annually.

This way, it serves as a reminder of each member's commitment and can be used when evaluating board member performance at the end of the year.

Hiring Your First Development Staff Member

As I said at the beginning of this book, fundraising is a team sport. That said, I've also tried to arrange the book to make it as easy as possible in case you're the only one currently fundraising for your organization.

But now, let's assume and break down the roles for the best-case scenario. Everyone is working together, and you have a full, small-shop development team—an executive director, development director, and administrative assistant. This way, you'll know the theory and be ready when your organization is ready to make this scenario a reality.

Role of the Executive Director

As executive director, you're the face of the organization. You should be front and center with donors, particularly major donors, as you're the one they want to meet and the one who can express best where the organization is headed.

You are also responsible for keeping everyone on the team accountable. I strongly suggest a short, weekly development team meeting. This is not to micromanage every project, but a quick check-in to find out what's on tap to move your organization forward. You can use the same two agenda items for this meeting each week:

◆ What did we do last week to move development (fundraising) forward? Who is responsible for the follow-up?

◆ What will we do this week or next week to move forward?

It is important to keep your team accountable and on track.

Role of the Development Director

In fundraising, the executive director's job is to be the puppet; the development director is the puppeteer. The development director does all the behind-the-scenes work, and the executive director does the entertaining. In other words, it's your development director's job to prepare you (and your board members) to go out on stage.

To do that, the development director:

◆ Helps identify, cultivate, solicit, and steward prospects

◆ Creates cultivation and solicitation plans for major donors, which are then generally executed by the executive director and a board member

◆ Carries out behind-the-scenes cultivation and facilitating meetings and next steps

◆ Plans out the solicitation and doing any research involved with that process

◆ Stewards donors

◆ Creates and oversees the execution of a comprehensive fundraising plan

Role of the Administrative Assistant

Administrative assistants, if you're fortunate enough to have one, are responsible for helping generate thank-you letters, pre- and post-meeting letters, and scheduling appointments when appropriate.

Every Interaction Matters

I once worked with an organization whose receptionist was always grouchy. Her bad mood came through loud and clear, both over the phone and in person. She treated people badly regardless of who they were—donors and board members included. She was a real problem for the agency's overall image!

In contrast, I once went to attend a committee meeting at a hospital. The staff member in front of the information desk not only gave me directions to the meeting room but insisted on walking me most of the way there, down several hallways. It was gracious of her and made quite an impression on me.

The hospital's staff turned a minor thing—finding a meeting room—into a positive and memorable experience.

While administrative duties may seem unimportant, they could make the difference between a receiving or not receiving a gift.

 stories from the real world

Also, your administrative assistant is generally the first person that others interact with when they contact or visit your organization. This interaction is very important to the overall "vibe" of your organization—in other words, it's the assistant's job to make friends for your nonprofit.

Supervising Your Development Staff

I know many well-meaning executive directors who are so overwhelmed that they leave all of the fundraising to the director of development. There are at least two problems with this approach. First, the development director can't raise as much money alone as the two of you can together. Second, many development directors, especially less-experienced ones, need benchmarks and supervision to stay on track.

Work closely with your development director to get asks out the door. Without micromanaging, have a list of goals for the development director to check off each month. As the executive director, it's up to you to ensure that your nonprofit's fundraising process and schedule of asks is being followed for every prospect.

Schedule weekly meetings with your development team. It could be you and your development staff member, plus the administrative assistant. If you don't have any staff, schedule a weekly meeting with your board president or development committee by phone. Have the two-item agenda I mentioned earlier, keep the meeting to ten minutes, and keep your team moving forward.

When to Hire Your First Development Staff Member

There comes a time in the life of every nonprofit when it's time to hire the first development staff member. How do you know when that time has come for your nonprofit? While there is no clear-cut answer, here are several important factors to consider:

◆ Why do you want to hire a development staff member? If it's to get you out of fundraising, that's not a good answer. Hopefully, your organization has grown to the point that you can afford an additional staff member and are also ready to expand your programs and services.

◆ Do you have the funding to pay the first year's salary? Organizations that expect development staff members to immediately raise their own salary (generally in unrestricted operating dollars) have unrealistic expectations from the start and are setting up the new staff members for failure. It's reasonable to expect your new development director to generate increased revenue during the first year—but it's not reasonable to expect enough unrestricted dollars to cover the position's salary and benefits.

◆ Have you discussed this new position with the board? The board should expect to work with the development staff member. If your board doesn't have a development committee, your development director will want to create one. The development director should be invited to participate in board meetings, and encouraged to work with board members to help leverage their networks and get involved with fundraising.

◆ Who will the new staff member report to? It's my strong belief that your top development staff member (or only development staff member, in this case) should report to you, to allow the two of you to work together closely. The only exception to this might be if you decide to hire a part-time grant writer or event planner who will not be working on any other types of fundraising.

Choosing the Right Person for Your Office

Before creating a job description and starting your search for the perfect candidate, first determine the type of person you're looking for. For example, if you're offering a small salary, you might want to consider someone straight from college who is eager, enthusiastic, hardworking, and willing to learn on the job. If you're seeking someone with more experience, you'll need to be prepared to pay more.

The next question to answer is, do you want a generalist with small-shop experience, or do you want someone with specific skills? If your current program staff can handle grant writing and event planning, you might want to consider someone who will expand your major gift program.

It's rare to find someone with the exact experience, skill set, and personality traits you're looking for. However, there are often several people who have many of the skills and personality traits that you would like, so review resumes and interview candidates with an open mind. (See the sample job description on the next page to get started with your search.)

Advertising Your Development Position

The most appropriate place to advertise a development position is in whatever publication or website most development people in your area use to look for jobs.

> ### Going from One to Two Development Staff Members
>
> When you get to the point of needing a second development staff member, it's probably because you're ready to grow in a particular area, such as grants or individual giving. There are many ways to expand your development office, and how you choose to do so will be based on the talents and skills you already have at your organization. Some organizations might want to consider hiring a grant writer, event planner, or major gifts director as their second development staff member.
>
>

Examples include:

◆ Association of Fundraising Professionals: *http://jobs.afpnet.org*

◆ Chronicle of Philanthropy: *http://philanthropy.com/jobs*

◆ IdeaList: *idealist.org*

Screening Resumes

You may already have a lot of experience screening resumes, but if you've never hired a development person before you need to know what to look for. By the way, some of the points below also apply to any position.

◆ Prior development experience. As basic as this is, I have received many resumes for development positions where the applicant has no prior development experience. This is fine if you're hiring someone straight from college, but not if you need someone with experience. However, there are now a lot of corporate executives making the switch to the nonprofit world. If you're open to the idea of a senior level person with sales or marketing experience, these can be great hires as well.

◆ Duration at prior jobs. Has the individual committed to organizations or bounced from job to job? Development staff members change jobs often, but you want someone who is going to stay at least three years. Ask why a candidate has left any position before three years, and whether or not you may call former employers.

Sample Job Description

When preparing your first development job description, take a look at existing job descriptions from similar organizations for an idea of appropriate language and reasonable requirements and qualifications. You can find these on any job search site. (See the section on "Advertising Your Development Position" for suggestions.)

XYZ Nonprofit Organization

Job Title: Director of Development

Job Location: New York, New York

Organization Description:

XYZ Organization has served homeless women and children in NYC for the last ten years. We are ready to hire our first development staff member and are looking for a terrific candidate to join our team.

Responsibilities Include:

◆ Creating initial development office, including policies and procedures

◆ Working with the executive director to establish development plan and goals

◆ Researching and identifying funding opportunities, including foundations, corporations, and individuals

◆ Reaching or exceeding annual fundraising goals

◆ Overseeing all administrative functions related to development, including data entry and data management, letter generation, etc.

◆ Working with board members and board committees, including development and events committees

Salary and Benefits:

◆ Salary is negotiable based on experience

◆ Generous benefit package with health insurance

Qualifications:

◆ Bachelor's degree required, master's degree preferred

◆ CFRE preferred

◆ Experience in a one-person development shop preferred

◆ Proven track record of fundraising with grant writing, events, and individual campaigns

◆ Excellent interpersonal and writing skills

◆ Passion for cause and mission

How to Apply: Send cover letter and resume to Joan Jones at XYZ at jjones@xyz.org.

◆ Promotions and increasing responsibility with matching titles. It's a positive sign when a candidate has received one or more promotions at a single organization or has had various jobs with increased levels of responsibility.

◆ Types of organizations. If an applicant has worked at only arts organizations, and your organization is a homeless shelter, you might want to discuss why the candidate wants to work in this new area and find out the person's level of commitment to your cause. The candidate must be genuinely interested in your mission to be an effective fundraiser.

Interviewing Development Staff

When you're interviewing development staff, think about the candidate from the perspective of your donors. With each candidate, ask yourself these questions:

◆ Do you want this person representing your organization to donors?

◆ Will this person fit with the culture of your organization?

◆ Is the candidate friendly? Does the person smile?

◆ Is the candidate a team player?

The questions you ask are crucial to getting a true picture of the candidate. Here are some sample interview questions to get you started:

◆ Why are you interested in this position?

◆ What experience in your background makes you qualified for this job?

◆ Why are you leaving your current position? Why did you leave former positions?

◆ Tell me about your development experience.

◆ How have you raised money in the past?

◆ What fundraising have you done that was successful and what not as successful? Why do you think one campaign was successful and the other not?

◆ What would you require to be successful in this job?

◆ Have you been involved in any continuing education? Are you interested in continuing education?

◆ How do you envision working with me (the executive director) in this position?

◆ Have you worked with a board or development committee before? In what capacity?

◆ What do you expect from board members? How would you work with them?

◆ What would you do during the first month on the job? First six months?

Salary and Benefits

Different organizations offer vastly different salaries and benefits depending on size, the type of services they provide, and region of the country they're located in.

AFP does an annual salary survey, which is probably your most useful reference when starting out. The amount you'll need to pay will largely depend on how much prior fundraising experience you're looking for, the industry you're in, and where you're located. For example, if you plan to hire someone without any prior experience straight out of college, you won't need to pay nearly as much as you will if you want someone with a Certified Fund Raising Executive (CFRE) credential who has been in the field for five or more years. Likewise, if your organization is in New York City, you'll be paying a higher salary than if you're located in South Dakota.

Of course, for whatever nonprofits lack in salary, they can often provide in other types of compensation, such as paid days off or flexibility in work hours. Since this is something you can offer without additional funding, I think it's an important place to be generous. I believe that a minimum of four weeks of vacation time will often substitute for a higher salary. Whenever possible, give people time off around the winter holidays or by closing early on Fridays during the summer as an added bonus.

Other possible benefits can include health insurance, retirement plans, flexible schedules, sick days, and other perks. Allowing some telecommuting is a huge benefit and highly desirable.

What to Expect from the First Year

There is an extremely high turnover rate among development professionals. One reason is that executive directors frequently have unrealistic expectations of what development staff can accomplish, especially with the tools and resources that they are given.

Set reasonable expectations at the onset, so you have something to measure success against at the end of the person's first year. For year one, some examples of good goals include:

> ### Budget Before You Hire
>
> In addition to salary and benefits, you need to have a budget for development activities. For example, what activities do you expect the new staff member to implement? Extra mailings cost money. Events cost money. Databases cost money. If you don't have a budget for your development staff member, you can't expect this person to implement many new fundraising activities or to raise much money.
>
>

◆ Establish a board development committee and meet four to six times. Create goals for board members.

◆ Work with board members to give and get. Have a plan to achieve 100 percent participation.

◆ Research and apply for ten new grants. Establish relationships with foundation staff members.

◆ Plan one event with a minimum of one hundred guests and at least five sponsors, which raises $20,000 or more. Follow up with VIPs from the event.

◆ Plan two house parties for prospective donors at the homes of board members.

◆ Send two new mailings to the database and invite them to join a monthly giving program.

◆ Enroll fifty people in a monthly giving club at a minimum of $10 per month.

◆ Create capacity for electronic correspondence and send five e-blasts.

◆ Help identify ten individual prospects and create cultivation plans for each. Help schedule meetings for them with board members and the executive director.

You'll notice that none of the above goals involves raising huge amounts of money. Instead, they're all about building a foundation that will allow your new hire to increase your organization's bottom line year after year.

To Recap

◆ Executive directors are ultimately responsible for fundraising for their organizations.

◆ Well-trained and selected board members will serve their organizations better than untrained board members.

◆ Board members need clear expectations, orientation, and ongoing training.

◆ Each staff member has an important role in fundraising.

◆ Supervision is critical to success.

◆ Know when to hire your first development staff member and what to look for.

◆ Create realistic expectations for your new development staff member and provide the tools for success.

Chapter Eleven

Putting It All Together: Keys to Success

In This Chapter

---→ Setting goals and sticking to them

---→ Staying on track

---→ Measuring success

---→ Strategies for staying motivated

As you know by now, *50 Asks in 50 Weeks* is about creating a simple development plan for busy small offices. However, if the plan isn't used by the people who created it, it isn't worth the paper it's written on. This final chapter outlines how to stay on track, follow your plan, and count and measure your success.

Develop Specific Goals and Objectives

If you're reading *50 Asks in 50 Weeks* you have one goal: raising more money. As I have discussed throughout this workbook, you can accomplish this goal by asking for gifts more frequently and asking in smarter, more efficient ways. To narrow down the overarching goal of raising more money, though, you first need to develop specific goals and objectives.

Before you do, I want you to think about how you've set goals in the past. Here are the two most common goals I've seen in nonprofits:

◆ Raise 5 percent more than last year.

◆ Raise enough money to cover the gap in the budget.

These are *terrible* ways to set goals. *Do not set goals like this!*

While raising 5 percent more than last year might seem like a smart goal, there are a lot of other factors that need to be considered, such as:

◆ Was last year a typical year or an anomaly?

◆ Do I have good reason to believe I will be able to raise more—and why? What will we do differently, and what will we keep the same?

Goals are general and broad in scope. When setting them, think about the number and quality of asks you will make. How many prospects do you have and what can you reasonably expect their giving levels to be? Do you have multiple prospects for each gift you expect to receive? Once you've decided on your goals, add a big number, like $10,000, $50,000, or even $100,000 more that you will raise this year. It helps to think big, and outside the box.

But don't forget: goals should be more than just a dollar figure. You should set other types of measurable goals, such as a higher number of contacts with donors.

Objectives are more specific. For each goal, list several objectives that will help you meet that goal, the staff or board member who is responsible for making it happen, and a deadline.

Finally, use a chart such as the one below to record your goals. Refer back to it monthly or quarterly to make sure you're on track.

Sample Goals and Objectives

Goal 1: Increase board participation in fundraising.

Objectives	Responsible Party	Deadline
100 percent participation	board president	February 1
2 board f/r trainings	development director	March and September

Goal 2: Enhance bulk solicitation program.

Objectives	Responsible Party	Deadline
Send 1 new mail appeal	development director	March
Send 4 e-newsletters	development director	Quarterly
Add notes to top donor appeals	executive director	October/March

Goals and objectives enable you to you know where to go and to determine when you've arrived. Review your goals and objectives regularly. If you don't accomplish one or more of them, it will be critical to determine the reason why.

Creating Your Fundraising Plan and Staying on Track

After completing all of the worksheets in this workbook, you should be able to condense your fifty asks onto the following one-page worksheet.

50 Asks in 50 Weeks Summary Sheet

Fill in each box with the name of a prospect or solicitation (such as an individual, a corporation, foundation, bulk mail solicitation, etc.) and the staff or board member responsible for the ask.

	Week 1 (1st Ask)	Week 2 (2nd Ask)	Week 3 (3rd Ask)	Week 4 (4th Ask)	5th Ask (Optional)
Example	M. Smith ED/Bd. Mbr.	Ford Grant DOD	GALA Sponsor DOD	Bank Request Bd. Mbr	email newsletter DOD
January					
February					
March					
April					
May					
June					
July					
August					
September					
October					
November					
December					

The only way I know of to truly keep on track and focused is by being accountable to someone else and setting public deadlines for yourself. As I mentioned in the previous chapter, schedule short, weekly development meetings with another person in your office or an outside accountability partner. This could be either the executive director, development director, board president, development committee chair, or a colleague at another organization. The only two agenda items for this weekly meeting are reviewing last week's ask and discussing the next ask. Knowing that you'll need to report your progress to someone else will light a fire under you like nothing else!

Measuring Success

There are many ways to measure success. The most obvious is the total number of dollars! However, there are many other measures to consider. For example:

◆ *Number of new donors.* Know the number of donors to any given campaign. How many people donated to your fall appeal this year and last year? How many came to your event?

◆ *Number of repeat donors.* Who gave again? Donor retention is crucial to fundraising. Are your donors so loyal to your cause and your organization that they will give again and again?

◆ *Number of lapsed donors.* How many donors did you lose? This is as or more important than the number you gained.

◆ *Average gift size.* Does your average rise or fall from year to year? Are there any outliers that are pulling your average up or down? What are the highest and lowest gifts?

◆ *Number of grants received.* It's not just the number of foundations you apply to, but the number of grants you actually receive, that matters.

Staying Motivated

Staying motivated and positive is the number one way I know to be a truly successful fundraiser.

Negativity becomes a self-fulfilling prophecy. If you believe that you won't raise any money, and then you act like you won't raise any money by sitting around moping at your desk, *you won't actually raise any money*. On the other hand, if you truly believe that you will raise money and act like it by going out and meeting with prospects, the money will follow.

For me, one of the most frustrating parts of being a one-person development shop was the isolation. Yes, I was surrounded by social workers and program people, but I didn't have anyone to brainstorm about fundraising ideas or who would

---

You Never Know When You'll Receive a Gift

The board president of an organization I once worked with told me an amazing story. She was in line at the grocery store and recognized the woman in front of her as a parent at her daughter's school. As they approached the front of the line, the woman realized that she had forgotten her wallet. Seeing that she only had a few items, the board president offered to pay them and gave her a $20 bill, knowing that she would probably never see the money again. She didn't have any paper to write down her name and phone number, but had a generic card from the organization and scribbled her name on that. A week went by, and the board president had forgotten all about the incident when she received a call from the executive director of her organization—who told her that there was a letter for her with a $20 bill in cash and a $200 check for the organization!

 stories from the real world

understand the ups and downs of my work. If you can, find a colleague or friend at another agency to help keep you motivated. Schedule a weekly pep talk and bounce ideas off each other. Tip: If your conversations start to get negative, find another friend.

Also, AFP has provided me with a fantastic network of professionals to consult and debrief with. Find a group of AFP fundraisers in your area to connect with on a regular basis. Better yet, join AFP, or a similar organization, and take part in at least one event to sharpen your skills! Here are some other organization you could join, as well:

◆ Association of Professional Researchers for Advancement (APRA). See *aprahome.org*.

◆ BoardSource. See *boardsource.org*.

◆ Grant Professionals Association (GPA). See *grantprofessionals.org*.

◆ Partnership for Philanthropic Planning (PPP). See *pppnet.org*.

◆ The Alliance for Nonprofit Management. See *allianceonline.org*.

◆ The Council for Advancement and Support of Education (CASE). See *case.org*.

Final Ideas for Asks

Here are some of the ideas for asks we've talked about in this book:

◆ Ask your board.

◆ Ask your clients.

◆ Ask your volunteers.

◆ Ask you board members to ask their friends, family, neighbors, and colleagues.

◆ Ask your staff to ask their friends, family, and neighbors.

◆ Ask on your website.

◆ Ask in your fall, spring, summer, and winter newsletters.

◆ Ask by bulk mail in a year-end appeal and throughout the year.

◆ Ask in monthly or quarterly electronic appeals.

◆ Ask in person, on the phone, and by mail.

◆ Ask on social networks—Facebook, LinkedIn, Twitter.

◆ Ask your vendors to be sponsors and supporters.

◆ Ask during Giving Tuesday and via other social giving platforms.

◆ Ask, ask, and ask some more!

I hope you have now identified at least fifty new prospects for your organization and learned at least a few new strategies for smart and frequent fundraising. If you implement the ideas in this workbook, please contact me to let me know what's working—and what isn't. Either way, I want to hear from you!

Good luck for a prosperous year in fundraising!

To Recap

◆ Set goals and objectives to raise more money.

◆ Stay motivated and positive about fundraising.

◆ Measure your success in order to know how you're doing.

◆ Meet with others in your office on a weekly basis to keep on track.

◆ For support, network with other fundraising professionals in your community and/or via a professional organization like AFP.

◆ Ask, ask, and ask some more!

Index

You also might be interested in our just-released *CharityChannel's Quick Guide to Developing Your Case for Support,* by Margaret Guellich and Linda Lysakowski.

*Charity*Channel's®
Quick Guide to™

Developing Your Case for Support

Margaret Guellich, CFRE
Linda Lysakowski, ACFRE

■ Learn what a case for support is, and isn't
■ Determine who should write your case for support
■ Prepare to gather all the information you need to write your case
■ Build a case that tells your story to your various "publics"

CharityChannel.com/bookstore

*Charity*Channel®
PRESS™

If you enjoyed this workbook, you'll want to pick up *Getting Started in Charitable Gift Planning: Your Guide to Planned Giving* and the companion *Getting Started in Charitable Gift Planning: The Resource Book,* published by CharityChannel Press.

Getting Started in Charitable Gift Planning

Your Guide to Planned Giving

Brian M. Sagrestano, JD, CFRE

Robert E. Wahlers, MS, CFRE

Your guide to planned giving that will:

■ Help you to understand gift planning in the 21st century

■ Outline the best infrastructure for a donor-focused gift planning program

■ Assist you in identifying and developing prospects for planned gifts

■ Guide you in creating a marketing plan to effectively grow your donor relationships

■ Provide helpful tips from the field

CharityChannel.com/bookstore

IN THE

Trenches™

RESOURCE

Getting Started in Charitable Gift Planning

The Resource Book

Brian M. Sagrestano, JD, CFRE

Robert E. Wahlers, MS, CFRE

Supplemental resources that assist you by:

- Explaining the basic tools of charitable gift planning
- Answering common gift planning questions
- Providing tools to build your gift planning program
- Defining key terms important in gift planning conversations

And so much more!

CharityChannel.com/bookstore

*Charity*Channel

PRESS

Did you know that CharityChannel Press is the fastest growing publisher of books for busy nonprofit professionals? Here are some of our most popular titles.

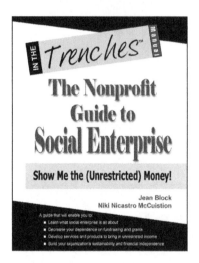

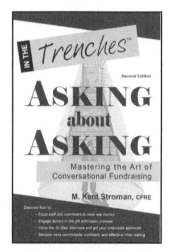

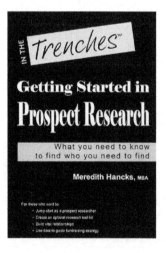

CharityChannel.com/bookstore

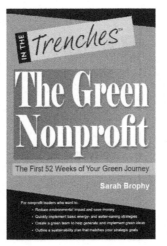

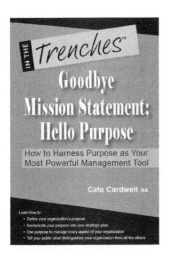

CharityChannel.com/bookstore

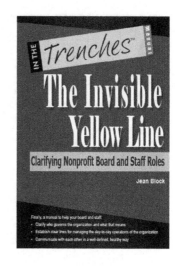

CharityChannel.com/bookstore

And now introducing **For the GENIUS® Press,** an imprint that produces books on just about any topic that people want to learn. You don't have to be a genius to read a **GENIUS** book, but you'll sure be smarter once you do!

Fundraising

Second Edition

for the GENIUS ™

A complete course in nonprofit fundraising

Linda Lysakowski

FOR THE GENIUS IN ALL OF US ™

ForTheGENIUS.com/bookstore

for the GENIUS ™
PRESS

Grantsmanship

for the GENIUS®

A master grantwriter and
a veteran funder reveal
the keys to winning grants

Goodwin Deacon
Ken Ristine

FOR THE GENIUS IN ALL OF US™

ForTheGENIUS.com/bookstore

PRESS

Nonprofit Board Service

for the GENIUS®

Find the right board, sharpen your skills, and become a stellar board member

Susan Schaefer, CFRE

Bob Wittig, MBA

FOR THE GENIUS IN ALL OF US™

ForTheGENIUS.com/bookstore

PRESS

Made in the USA
Middletown, DE
15 July 2021